MW01170636

TABLE OF CONTENTS

ABOUT

I have no particular qualifications to write a book on the subject of citizenship. That is, in fact, the point. I have never been a particularly activist person. I have never previously written anything longer than my master's thesis. And I certainly lack the intellectual ability to contribute any original thinking on this topic. If any credit is due, it is thanks to the academic, scientific, and research communities and their many impressive people and organizations whose thinking has contributed to this effort. All misstatements and misinterpretations of their work are solely mine. I trust that readers will look beyond my deficiencies and view this as it is—an attempt by a citizen to educate himself to the point where he can act as a responsible citizen.

While the opinions on this site are mine alone, this work has been inspired by many people I have had the fortune to meet over the years. To my teachers at the Portsmouth Abbey School, I remain grateful for their patience, expert instruction, and insistence that I succeed. Poor students can succeed when the three "R"s are relentlessly taught in a community that demands "reverence, respect, and responsibility." To my colleagues in the human capital practice at Mercer, I am particularly grateful for their insights on human development, incentives, and fact-based analysis. I also thank a succession of fine leaders who gave me progressively more opportunity (and responsibility!) during my 35-year career in consulting. Most of all, I am grateful for the "global perspective" provided to me by the faculty, my classmates, and fellow alumnae at the graduate Master of Arts program at the Fletcher School of Law and Diplomacy at Tufts University. Not only are these many of the smartest people I have ever met, they are also, as a group, model global citizen patriots.

Finally, I wish to thank my parents for the gifts of education and just the right amount of guidance. And love and thanks to my wonderful wife and daughters who provide, every day, a reality check and the needed support that allows me to pursue my dreams.

INTRODUCTION

Responsible Citizens and Responsive Government:
The Case for Global Citizen Patriots

Americans are not model citizens. The majority of us don't regularly vote, and our opinions are often informed more by social and economic position than through critical evaluation of issues. These problems are reinforced and exacerbated by media bias, commercial influences, and secondary and tertiary education curricula that do not prepare us to take responsibility for the duties of citizenship. Our inability to be responsible citizens within our own country means that we are less than responsible global citizens, as well.

Recognizing the challenges inherent in broad-based citizenship, the Founding Fathers of our democracy wisely set in place a system of representation designed to balance the expressed, and often short-term, needs of various citizen constituencies with the broader, and longer-term, goals of society. The foundation of this representative leadership is the need for these representatives to work for all the people. Alas, it is clear that our representatives no longer work for us. Rather, they are biased by corrupt (but technically legal) processes that permit money from special interest groups to influence policy. This bias is pervasive throughout the entire system of representative elections, re-elections, and the gerrymandering of voter districts. As Harvard Professor Lawrence Lessig states, "the system is rigged." He is correct.

This combination of citizen irresponsibility and representative system failure is toxic to the aspirations of our Founding Fathers. It doesn't have to be this way. An activist approach to citizen responsibilities coupled with changes to the representative system that allow our representatives to work for all citizens can restore, and extend, the vision of our founders.

This book focuses on the conditions and policies necessary for effective representative citizen rule. History teaches us many lessons about empires, citizenship, and the best ways to balance constitutional values, democracy, and capitalism. These lessons suggest ways forward that require extensive debate and citizen engagement. Indeed, our Founding Fathers, the authors of our visionary Constitution, recognized that periodic debate and change would be necessary. To some, constitutional debate is heresy. However, we would be wise to recall that Thomas Jefferson wrote in 1816, "some men look at constitutions with sanctimonious reverence, and deem them, like the Ark of the Covenant, too sacred to be touched. They ascribe to men of the preceding age a wisdom more than human, and suppose what they did to be beyond amendment." Jefferson went on to write, "laws and institutions must go hand in hand with the progress of the human mind." American citizens, drawing on their history of patriotic activism, are the essential catalyst for the continued evolution of the American Dream.

"Mad as Hell"

The first chapter of this book describes two fundamental failures of American representative government. If there is anything that Americans seem to agree on, it is that our national representatives have failed us in recent years. Look no further than congressional approval rates. The inability to govern through logical debate and compromise is a direct consequence of partisan, money-driven politics. Until this changes, we will be unable to objectively confront the major issues of our time: environmental protection, security, economic progress, poverty alleviation, opportunity for all, racial and economic inequality, immigration, and so on. If America is to protect and advance its interdependent system of constitutional values, democracy, and capitalism, our representatives need to work for all. Redefining their roles, responsibilities, accountabilities, and incentives is essential.

However, reducing or eliminating the money-driven bias of our representatives will not ensure that citizens have the tools and information they need to transcend their social, economic, and historical biases in ways that promote the general interest. We live in an incredibly complex world. It is beyond human capacity for citizens to be versed in all matters of public policy. The time commitment required for activism on even a couple of large-scale issues is daunting. So, by necessity we delegate this policy making to our representatives. However, this delegation in no way relieves citizens from the obligations of informed voting, participation in debate, and holding our government representatives accountable to "we the people." It is time for a bill of citizen responsibilities to complement our Bill of Rights. Chapter 1 recommends two changes designed to facilitate informed, activist citizens and clear the obstacles to effective representation. Both citizens and their representatives need to do their jobs. It is easy to be mad about the current state of affairs. However, only responsible citizen patriots can ensure responsible government.

Empires Lost and Values Gained

Chapter 2 describes the rationale for American global leadership. Here again, the lessons of history can help define the values and the structures that will make this leadership most beneficial to citizens everywhere. It is unclear if the post–World War II period of US economic, military, and cultural hegemony will end anytime soon. However, only America presently enjoys the soft and hard power to influence the advancement of an improved global system of, for example, economic development, security, rule of law, environmental protections, and essential human freedoms and values. American citizens have not always embraced the need for global leadership. This reticence is increasingly futile in the face of the relentless forces of globalization. Like it or not, America will lead, either in a planned and directed manner with clear objectives or in a reactionary and erratic manner. In its best moments, America has helped the world achieve great things. There is a plethora of opportunity for America to model policies and behaviors that will pull, rather than push, the world to a better place. America's citizens must have a global perspective. We must do the right things—for ourselves and for others.

Desperately Seeking Citizen Patriots

Chapter 3 defines the terms *citizens* and *patriots* and explains why both are essential to effective change and ongoing progress. Our Constitution and Bill of Rights are always the starting point (and, for some, the ending point) of discussions concerning changes to our democratic systems. But where is the Bill of Responsibilities that defines the requirements of citizenship? Moreover, what values underscore these requirements? Clarity on linkage between patriotic values and citizen responsibilities is a fundamental engine of change. Obtaining this clarity requires that we take a candid look at ourselves and come to terms with the myths of America. Millions of American citizens have died to perpetuate the American Dream both at home and abroad. They did their job as global citizen patriots, and we honor their sacrifices when we, as concerned global citizens, apply that same altruistic patriotism to create a better world. This chapter defines the job of global citizen patriots in a fast-changing global society.

Balancing Constitution, Democracy, and Capitalism

Chapter 4 discusses the interdependent system of constitution, capitalism, and democracy needed to support citizen patriots. While this system seems, after centuries of often-disastrous trial and error, to have emerged as the best combination, it is clear that creating balance between the three is difficult. In America, for example, crony capitalism has negatively influenced the effectiveness of our democracy and has contributed to potentially destabilizing inequalities. This, combined with the failure of representatives to do their jobs in the face of perverse incentives, poses great risks to the ideals that served as the foundation of historical American progress and success. For example, Russia has a well-conceived constitution but fails to follow it in either practice or in spirit. While there has been a marked increase in the number of countries that declare themselves democracies, there is a wide variation in their democratic performance. So, both the form and the substance of constitutional, capitalistic, and democratic models (and how they work together) are important. When imbalances occur, people suffer and die. Citizen understanding of how these systems can work together should go hand in hand with the patriotic zeal to push for ongoing and system-wide improvement. This chapter discusses what our system is for. What are our values, and what do we value? How do our democracy and capitalism combine to reinforce our values? How do we rebalance the system to continuously adapt?

Ensuring Leaders, Not Lackeys

Chapter 5 defines the first of two essential changes required if Americans are to eliminate the corruption that is presently paralyzing effective policy. The causes and effects of representative corruption are discussed primarily in terms of their corrosive effect on the objectivity and performance of our elected representatives. America enjoys a uniquely powerful combination of capital resources. These need to be managed and deployed in the best possible ways if we are to optimize our society and its global impact. Managing these capital resources is the primary task of our representatives. Finding the best possible representative talent, clearly defining their responsibilities, and altering their compensation, incentives, and oversight are the critical performance levers that can make our elected representatives leaders of citizen patriots rather than the lackeys of special interests.

Bridging the Gap: The Need for Short-Term Thinking

Chapter 6 states the need for short-term thinking. The 2016 election process is a great opportunity to initiate change in the behavior of our representatives, the political parties, the presidential candidates, and, most importantly, citizens themselves. The special interests that corrupt our system fear large voter turnouts and candidates who disdain large contributions from those special interests. As voters, we will make better choices if we vary our information sources and make genuine efforts to see all sides of the issues. Objectivity and information balance are foundational if voters are to choose well. Let's identify and build upon the many things we agree on rather than be used as pawns to highly partisan and narrow issues. Finally, candidates must articulate clear programs to improve the public/private partnership between government and business in ways that ensure long-term national fiscal responsibility while promoting human capital development and opportunity for all. The 2016 election is an opportunity to initiate change—and demonstrate the power of global citizen patriots.

Reality TV for Twenty-First-Century Global Citizen Patriots

Chapter 7 describes the long way to formation of an informed and activist citizenry. Citizenship is the most important job in an effective democracy, and it should have accountabilities, rewards, and penalties that ensure the job is well done. But citizens are created, not born.

Changes to our education system are only the start. We also need to find practical ways to amend and update our Constitution while engaging the broad citizenry in the debate. Jefferson and the Founding Fathers knew this would be necessary. We have done it in the past (although not in decades), and it is time to reform at least two areas of our Constitution that inhibit citizen performance and bias the performance of our representatives. Changes to the Constitution are not to be taken lightly. Potential changes need to be focused on essential improvements to the overall system of constitutional values, representative democracy, and capitalistic structures. Changes need to be thoughtfully and publicly debated in forums that reach and engage multiple constituents. These ongoing debates can be structured as mini constitutional conventions focused initially on two constitutional issues: citizen and representative performance. Over time, this type of forum can be expanded to debate the most important non-constitutional issues, as well. This would be great reality television. Jefferson would be proud!

Quo Vadis? The Policy Debates

The constitutional debates suggested in Chapter 7 and their outcomes will not address the major policy issues of society. Chapter 8 invites reader input. Have a broader list of non-constitutional issues for debate? Let's hear from you on the Global Citizen Patriots website (globalcitizenpatriots.com). Reader comments and ongoing discussion can help ensure that everything from the basic questions of representative and citizen underperformance to policy alternatives are fact-based and seen from a range of viewpoints. In addition to focusing attention on a comprehensive number of issues, these debates will ideally promote discussion of the pros and cons of various policy alternatives.

Open and balanced discussions are anathema to today's special interest groups. And that is why they need to occur. The outcomes of these debates can provide citizens with the decision tools needed to take more informed and balanced positions. We will never agree on all the issues, even with the most informed and most objective citizen education processes. It is doubtful that Fox News or MSNBC will agree on many policy issues, and both media sources represent a point of view. But all Americans would benefit from regular and additional sources of fact-based and balanced information. Through debate and the availability of additional media and educational system influences, our elected representatives can act based upon the input of "we the people." Let's start the discussion.

Additional chapters may be written online based on input to the website from readers. A benefit of an online book format is that it can encourage readers to react to what is written, suggest alternatives, and provide new ideas and thinking. The original goal of this project was to determine if American citizens are capable of performing the duties of citizenship. After four years of research and thought, the author remains optimistic that global citizen patriots can be the impetus for change that benefits all. The past four years have been well spent, an active civics lesson that has provided more questions than answers but a growing confidence that the emergence of global citizen patriots can lead America and the world to a better future. The author looks forward to your participation, advice, and ideas.

Common Sense for the Twenty-First Century

In 1776, Thomas Paine published *Common Sense,* arguing for an independent America governed by citizens through their elected representatives. It was designed to enlist Americans in the cause to not only throw off British rule but to establish a new system of values, democracy, and commercialism that favored merit and talent over hereditary privilege. Paine's short pamphlet was widely read and a factor in mobilizing the sentiment that led to the Declaration of Independence, the Revolution, and the formation of the United States. Most of all, it was Paine's attempt to offer a case for an alternative to English government that "is unconnected with any Party, and under no sort of Influence public or private, but the influence of reason and principle."[1]

Today, America faces new challenges caused by corrupting influences on our representatives and a seeming loss of attention by voters to arguments of reason and principle. The inability of Congress to govern, caused by the influence of money combined with voters' sense of disempowerment, requires the application of common sense for the twenty-first century. Further, the ever-increasing impact of globalization requires Americans to rethink the very concept of independence in an interdependent world. America's present citizens will determine our legacy. There is much to think about and debate. The author hopes that the information, suggestions, and questions posed in this book contribute to that debate and the decisions that will define America's legacy to future citizens and the world.

---

1 Thomas Paine. *Common Sense.* Philadelphia: W. and T. Bradford [1776]; Bartleby.com, 1999. www.bartleby.com/133/. (Accessed August 27, 2016).

CHAPTER 1:
"MAD AS HELL"

Citizens failed. Bring back the good old days of Stalin.

We Should Be Mad

In the signature moment of the 1976 movie *Network*, television anchor Howard Beale, played by Peter Finch, declares "I'm as mad as hell, and I'm not going to take it anymore!"

In Beale's world, things are bad and everything is crazy. People are out of work, the dollar is falling in value, homicide and crime are rampant, the air is unfit to breathe and food unfit to eat. All the while, Americans sit in their homes, segregated by income, ethnicity, religious doctrine, and other forms of social differentiation, hoping that the ills of society will leave them alone. Beale, plagued by low ratings, feels devalued as his network increasingly stresses sensationalism and entertainment rather than objective news reporting. His frustrations boil over in this classic rant as Beale asserts, "You've got to get mad. You've got to say, I am a human being . . . . My life has value."

Network's view of television seems less satirical today. Unwittingly, Beale might have become the first realty television host. His rant caused his network's ratings to soar but, in the end, only resulted in management pressure for even more ranting and less actual reporting. Forty years later, our reasons to be "mad as hell" are different yet every bit as maddening. Frustration and concern is everywhere. Is this frustration and concern misplaced?

Consider some of the evidence. America is the wealthiest country if one considers its aggregate assets in human capital (for example, labor supply, health, education, and the knowledge and skills that contribute to productive work), natural capital (water, energy, arable land, and conservation processes that sustain our ability to produce goods and services, etc.), manufactured capital (tools, machines, and other capital equipment and buildings that facilitate efficient output), social capital (communities, schools, and other forms of civil society that help us live and work together), and financial capital (the ability to monetize and trade the other capital assets in ways that spur investment and production). So why is it that the country with the best combination of capital assets:

- Is sixteenth on the World Social Progress Index, a measure of a country's performance on basic human needs, well-being, and opportunity?[1]

- Ranks sixteenth in an index of "most democratic" countries?[2]

- Is 46th in life expectancy?[3]

- Ranks first in health care spending, at 17.1% of gross domestic product (GDP), roughly 5% higher than other developed countries, with poorer health-care outcomes and without universal health insurance?

- Has a child poverty rate approaching 25%, thirty-fourth out of thirty-five developed nations?[4]

- Has a public school system that spends markedly more per student for those in wealthy communities versus those in the poorest communities?[5]

- Doesn't rank in the top twenty-eight of countries in terms of press freedom?[6]

- Doesn't make the top twenty in terms of women representatives in government?[7]

---

1 *The Economist Pocket World in Figures* 2016 edition (London, Profile Books, 2016) p. 31

2 Ibid., p. 41

3 Ibid., p. 80

4 "Measuring Child Poverty," UNICEF (May, 2012) p. 3

5 "On the Charts (Public)," *Westchester Magazine* (March 2013) p. 88

6 *Economist Pocket World*, p. 96

7 Ibid., p. 41

- Has a government that has performed "well below average"[8] when compared to the performance of leading democratic nations?

- Puts up with gun homicide rates that are three to four times that of other developed countries?[9]

- Has citizens whose average satisfaction with life ranks fifteenth when compared with other advanced industrial nations?[10]

- Has voting participation rates of approximately 40% for midterm elections and 60% in presidential election years with even lower participation among the young and the poor?

- Suffers from growing total income (the total of labor and investment capital) inequality where the top 10% have a 50% share of US national income versus a share of 20% for the bottom 50%?[11]

- Ranks sixteenth in public corruption, behind the majority of western European countries, Canada, Australia, New Zealand, and Singapore?[12]

Why, with all of our advantages in capital, have we not addressed these collective deficiencies? Being "mad as hell" does not change things. Like the patriots who took the responsibilities and risks of creating our country, we need to re-create that patriotic citizenship if we are to be

---

8 Derek Curtis Bok, *The Politics of Happiness: What Government Can Learn from the New Research on Well-Being* (Princeton, NJ, Princeton University Press, 2010) p. 184

9 "UNODC Homicide Statistics 2012," UNODC, 2012

10 Bok, p. 24

11 Thomas Piketty, *Capital in the Twenty-First Century* (Cambridge, MA, Belknap Press of Harvard University Press, 2014) p. 249

12 2015 Corruption Perceptions Index (Transparency International) from NPR 1/27/2016 article, "What Were the Least (and Most) Corrupt Countries in 2015?"

true to, and enhance, the Founding Fathers' vision. Our future, and the world's, depends on it. At present, we are, like the Russian ladies in the previous Saint Petersburg, Russia, photo, longing for a past that never really existed (the babushkas are advocating the return of Stalinism) while blaming outside enemies (in this case, the United States) for problems that are really failures of citizen awareness and participation. The babushkas, and we, need to do better.

Two Failures

This book focuses on two critical failures that inhibit America's ability to perform its essential global leadership role in progressing liberty and justice for all. Failing to address either issue compromises our ability to use current preeminence to forge a better world for current and future generations. Attempting to attack any of the problems listed in the previous section without setting in place a firm foundation for change will result in solutions that are piecemeal, short term, and less than optimally effective. Even worse, our inability to honestly discuss and debate the pros and cons of alternatives empowers partisan groups who represent uncompromising positions. The success of candidates like Trump and Sanders in the 2016 presidential election process attests to the deep frustration of Americans with an intractable political status quo that fails to deliver effective representative democracy or to reasonably distribute economic progress. Yet we seem unable to channel this frustration and energy into a process of reform. The 2016 election is an opportunity for candidates to commit to overcoming moneyed interests. However, the tenor and dishonesty of the debate cannot improve unless citizens insist on it. Yet we as citizens, and by extension our

representatives in Congress, are ill prepared and improperly incentiv-
ized to perform as citizens.

How have we gotten to this point?

Failure of Representatives to Lead the Evolution of Our Constitutional Ideals

First, we have failed to update, on a timely and systematic basis, the
ideals inscribed in our Constitution, its Amendments, and the Bill of
Rights. Rather, we often seem to get to the right place only after exhausting all other alternatives. This is surely not the best way to adapt to a
continually and fast-changing world. As the scholar Yuval Levin has
noted, we are "confused about what liberty and progress really mean
and require."[13] This confusion applies to Democrats, Republicans, and
those who do not align with either of the two major political parties. As
Levin states, the "conservative party is confused about what it should
conserve and our liberal or progressive party is confused about what it
should advance. The two are not misguided in exactly the same way, but
both tend toward radically deficient visions of the life of a liberal society." Assuming that most can agree that greater human liberty requires
progress, and that "such progress is achievable by arranging our laws
and institutions so as to best enable people's freedom to choose,"[14] it
seems logical to revisit the necessary limits to individual freedom (and
the structures that support those limits) that promote human progress
and the advancement of civil cooperation and stability.

---

13 Yuval Levin, "Taking the Long Way," *First Things*, (Oct. 2014) p. 1

14 Ibid., p. 2

Our Founding Fathers debated these issues over two hundred years ago. Their work was remarkable, but it is never finished. By definition, ideals are dynamic. The *Random House Dictionary of the English Language* defines the term *ideal* as "a conception of something in its perfection," "a standard of perfection or excellence," "an ultimate object or aim of endeavor, esp. one of high or noble character," and "something considered as a standard to strive toward." Ideals are goals that are aspirations, requiring ongoing evaluation and alteration. The authors of the Constitution could not have anticipated the material, economic, social, cultural, or political changes that two centuries have brought. They knew this at the time and provided for ongoing amendment and change. This is the fundamental job of elected representatives.

It is time for a new group of constitutional representatives to confirm and update American ideals, reach compromise conclusions, and bring them to the American citizenry for debate and action. However, before this can happen, citizen patriots must require that representatives work for "we the people" and not other interests. One of the author's former business colleagues was fond of saying, "nothing happens until somebody sells something." Similarly, nothing can happen until our representatives in government work for us. Tired of congressional gridlock? Sick over our inability to act on many of the issues important to our society? This dysfunction is the result of a representative government that is no longer representing its citizens. Now that is something to get mad about! And it is the first of the two critical problems we have to fix.

Failure of Citizens: Rights Require Responsibilities

However, there is a second, equally fundamental, problem. Citizens must participate in the evolution of these ideals. Here, the evidence suggests that citizens themselves fail to live up to even the basic responsibilities of citizenship. Yes, we do pay taxes, perform military service, generally obey the law, and, at least sometimes, vote. But do citizens' responsibilities end there? Where is the Bill of Responsibilities to balance the Bill of Rights? Immigrants seeking US citizenship learn that their responsibilities also include supporting and defending the Constitution, staying informed and participating in their communities, and respecting the rights, beliefs, and opinions of others. But surely the list of responsibilities goes beyond these items. Should the education system take additional responsibility to enable the critical thinking skills necessary to objectively evaluate a range of positions? Should curricula include more education focused on informing and developing model citizens? What are the responsibilities of media, non-government organizations, and the education system to help citizens understand and evaluate different points of view? Should citizens be responsible for cultivating a more global perspective? Taking this last issue alone, should citizens have the responsibility, as suggested by the Global Citizens Initiative,[15] to:

- Understand one's own perspective and the perspectives of others on global issues?

- Respect the principle of cultural diversity?

- Make connections and build relationships with people from other countries and cultures?

15 Global Citizens Initiative.org

- Understand global issues, the ways in which the people's and the countries of the world are inter-connected and interdependent, and to advocate for more effective global equity and justice?

Is it time for a Bill of Responsibilities that clearly defines the role of a citizen? Should citizens lose some of their rights or even their citizen status if they fail to exercise their responsibilities? How do we ensure that citizens, their representatives, and the government remain true to those responsibilities? How can a Bill of Responsibilities best define the ideals that we want to shape the future? What values and beliefs need to be baked into these responsibilities? These are essential questions of value that need debate and resolution.

Responsible Citizens Are Patriots, Not Populists

The failure of citizens to be responsible to collective ideals and a shared vision of the future defaults to the current system of extreme democracy gone wrong in which committed and well-funded special interests compromise our government representatives. Further, voter frustration with representative failure results in populist efforts to circumvent the representative system with referendums and other forms of direct representation that can be detrimental to society. Look no further than California's experience with referendums, recalls, ballot initiatives, and propositions. Consider the impact of the most notable of these, known as Proposition 13. Passed via voter referendum in 1978 (it was easy to sell—what taxpayer doesn't want to reduce taxes?), it cut the property tax rate from an average of 2.6% to 1% in every California county. In addition, Proposition 13 limited the amount of future increases in the property tax rate and prevented legislators from making up shortfalls in other areas. The net effects of this populist revolt were devastating to both representative democracy and to public services in California. Since Prop 13, California's public education system has deteriorated, its roads, bridges, and parks have been neglected, and its government representatives have been disempowered by increasing numbers of initiatives that have qualified for the ballot (74 between 2000 and 2010).[16]

This is not what the Founding Fathers had in mind. James Madison wrote, "pure democracies have ever been spectacles of turbulence and contention."[17] "Madison understood that a large and diverse nation would necessarily have many antagonistic minority factions, or special interests in today's language."[18] Hence, a Constitution was written that filters the preferences of these populist groups through a Senate and a House of Representatives that, together, are charged with balancing the various interests in ways that suit the general good. It is this balance of citizen involvement (but not control) and representative independence (but with accountability) that has allowed our Constitution to endure and be a model for others. So, our second failure is not a Constitutional failure. Rather, it is a failure of citizens to do their job. Combining this with representatives compromised by special interests is fatal to the vision of our founders.

---

16 "The People's Will," *The Economist* (April 23, 2011) p. 4

17 Ibid., p. 5

18 Ibid., p. 6

Two Solutions

Achieving consensus on updated ideals is a difficult task in a society with strongly held and diverse beliefs. Similarly, reforming our representative democracy—an immediate need—through increased citizen awareness and activism requires a long-term perspective with initial steps that will remove the most prominent barriers to change. Channeling our "mad as hell" emotions into patriotic citizenship (as opposed to partisan politics) can drive reform. It is up to us, and there are two suggested first steps.

Define What Twenty-First-Century America Stands For

Any discussion of updating ideals that will impact our Constitution, its Amendments, and/or the Bill of Rights will only be manageable if there is a clear goal. This goal should be to add a Bill of Responsibilities that balances our well-described individual rights with community responsibilities that have for too long remained both limited and ill defined. In the broadest sense, the goal is to update our ideals (using this Bill of Responsibilities) to better balance the freedoms of individuals with the responsibilities of these individuals to collective societal progress (society in this context should be viewed as local, national, and global). As the InterAction Council proposed in 1997, "it is time to talk about human responsibilities."[19] By incorporating the discussion of ideals under the mantra of broad human responsibilities, and by equating citizen and human responsibilities, it should be possible to make progress quickly.

---

19 The InterAction Council, "A Universal Declaration of Human Responsibilities," p. 1

In fact, the idea of a Bill of Responsibilities is hardly new. There are many well-conceived versions already in existence that can serve as a starting place for debate. For example, the Universal Declaration of Human Responsibilities, authored by the InterAction Council, provides a very good start with well-considered responsibilities in the categories of Fundamental Principles for Humanity, Nonviolence and Respect for Life, Justice and Solidarity, Truthfulness and Tolerance, and Mutual Respect and Partnership. The breadth of signatures to this declaration (including a broad range of national, religious, economic, environmental, and business leaders from around the world) suggests that the basic principles can be agreed upon. Translating these into citizen- and country-specific responsibilities, accountabilities, and enforcement methods are more difficult, but progress on these can be made over a longer time frame as long as the principles are established. Certainly, the debate on these issues will be the highest form of reality television!

Enable Our Representatives to Work for All Citizens

Adding a well-vetted agreement on citizen (and by extension, national) responsibilities only solves one problem. How should we address the failure that our representatives no longer work for us? Incentives matter. As the author's former Mercer colleagues tell their corporate clients, your organization becomes (over time) what it rewards. Transferring this basic economic logic to the US Congress, the evidence is clear that the behaviors of our representatives are driven by the ways in which they are rewarded. I doubt that many of the best and brightest CEOs of successful organizations would be attracted to careers in congressional service based on the current pay for these jobs. If we want the best possible representatives, we should pay them a wage that is competitive with wages for top talent. However, at the same time, we need to cut off the flow of monies and non-monetary influencers that bias their legislative work in favor of those who provide campaign contributions, high-paying future jobs, and other benefits that are needed for election and reelection campaigns. Publicly funded elections (at the congressional and presidential levels) may cost the taxpayers more (particularly if we start paying them like top talent), but increased effective governance and reduced legislative bias are fundamental to a well-functioning democracy.

Fixing the representative rewards system is necessary, but by itself it is not a sufficient condition for change. There must be clarity on the roles and responsibilities of representatives. Increased focus on, and accountability to, well-articulated goals that balance constituent preferences with overall national (and international) goals is essential if we are to evaluate representative performance and their suitability for, for example, reelection. In addition, voter districts need to be altered to reduce the compromising impact of gerrymandering on the concept of majority-determined elections. These and other ways to reduce bias in our representative system are detailed in Chapter 4.

The Current Opportunity for Global Citizen Patriots

The time for citizens to raise these essential reform issues is now. Elections are a powerful lever for citizens to insist on changes. Overcoming partisan and party politics is only a start. Candidates must be able to suggest both short- and long-term alternatives to our present dysfunction that improve liberty, justice, and opportunity for all. Building walls in an ever-globalizing world (Trump), giving away free benefits without proper financing (Sanders), and the willingness to accept large contributions from special interests (Clinton) are signs of candidate inadequacy. Citizens and their representatives deserve better. Now is the time for global citizen patriots who demand more.

We should be mad as hell. Let's channel that anger into patriotic citizenship.

Much of the remainder of this book is dedicated to defining the roles and responsibilities of global citizen patriots and their representatives and the ways in which important changes can be advanced. However, these roles and responsibilities cannot be formed in isolation without consideration of the realities of globalization. America may be, at present, the most powerful nation in many ways. But, as a country, we have diminishing sole control over our jobs, our security, our finances, our environment, our technologies, and most other factors. We are part of a changing world that does not conform to the preferences of even its most powerful member. History records that some of America's most meaningful global interventions (in the twentieth century, for example, the world wars, and the rebuilding of Europe and Japan) have been not only the best demonstration of American values and altruism, but these investments in global stability and prosperity have been of considerable benefit to Americans, as well. This framework of global opportunity is an important context as we consider the roles and responsibilities of citizen patriots. So, before moving on, we need to consider the evolving geopolitical position of the United States, understand the lessons of history, and examine the global opportunity for the United States to provide leadership that will shape a better world for all.

CHAPTER 2:
EMPIRES LOST AND VALUES GAINED

Sunset or dawn? Doing the right thing.

For many in the United States, a country with a history of self-determination and self-dependence, it is difficult to accept that our fate is increasingly tied to influences outside our borders. More and more, it is necessary to partner with others to address problems and opportunities. As David Held states, "the very possibility of national economic policy is, accordingly, problematic."[1] Beyond national economic policy, other areas of necessary multilateral cooperation include, for example, the fight against terrorism, cyber security, disaster relief and humanitarian aid, production and financial transactions, trade, pollution control and abatement, limiting the proliferation of weapons of mass destruction and potentially destructive technologies, and protection of fisheries and other wildlife commons. Much has been done in terms of creating

---

1 David Held, *Models of Democracy* (Stanford, CA, Stanford University Press, 2006) p. 297

cooperative institutions designed to operate across borders. The United Nations, the European Union, NATO, the International Criminal Court, the World Bank, the International Monetary Fund, and the World Trade Organization were all created to address issues that transcend country borders. In addition, numerous non-government organizations (NGOs) exist to address problems that often involve multinational cooperation. Examples of some of the largest of these include Doctors Without Borders, the Red Cross/Red Crescent, UNICEF, Oxfam, Care International, Catholic Relief Services, Aga Khan Development Network, Save the Children, and Plan International. These institutions exist because there is a need for them. However, they often lack adequate authority and the resources to influence, coordinate, and enforce common decisions. The historian Niall Ferguson concludes that, "There is, in truth, only one power capable of playing an imperial role in the modern world, and that is the United States. Indeed, to some degree it is already playing that role."[2]

Why should America play such a role? Why should the United States bear the burden of leadership? What is it, other than economic and military might, that suggests that America is best positioned to lead? What is in it for our citizens? How does this impact the responsibilities and behaviors of citizens and their representatives? America may be playing the "imperial" role unconsciously and by default, but we need to understand why and to what purpose. The lessons of history can instruct us. And our constitutional values need to guide us. Above all, the role we play in the world is a basic question of values.

---

2 Niall Ferguson, *Empire: The Rise and Demise of the British World Order and the Lessons for Global Power* (New York, Basic, 2003) p. 367

Empires and Values

In *Empire,*[3] the historian Niall Ferguson documents the lessons learned from the nineteenth- and twentieth-century history of the British Empire. Nineteenth-century Britain was the globally dominant power in many of the same ways that America is today. Ferguson convincingly argues that it was the British Empire that most shaped the modern world, not through solely military or economic dominance. Rather, the enduring and positive influences of the British Empire were due more to its liberal values and economic and democratic systems and the way Britain consciously transferred these to their colonies. Equally important, it was the way the British unraveled their empire during the twentieth century that truly cemented a lasting and positive legacy.

Examples of Britain's balance of liberal values and democratic systems, and their positive effects on the world, are evidenced by their leadership in:

- Abolition of slavery and the slave trade and advancement of the concept of free labor

- Exporting European ideas, including the concepts of universal education and opportunity for all

- Advancing individual rights balanced by parliamentary, collective representation

---

3 Ibid.

- Instilling humanitarian values, ethics, and morality that, while based on English religious values, provided their subjects with Enlightenment-based rights and protections

- Sharing the support systems of modernization and liberal capitalism, including health care, a hearty legal framework, food production, and manufacturing

- Developing the first global system of communication

- Promulgating English as the common global language of commerce

- Promoting or at least accepting self-determination by its colonies once the empire could no longer support itself

Certainly military and economic strength gave Britain the hard and soft power it needed to influence its colonies. But it was the ability to balance this hard and soft power with humanitarian values that, in the long run, differentiates Britain.

When Values Fail

This is not to understate the failures of British hegemony. Britain's expansion in the eighteenth and nineteenth centuries had the deleterious effect of launching a century of colonial expansion by other colonial powers. Much of this turned out tragically. Ferguson provides telling examples. The Belgian colonization of the Congo "operated on the basis of slave labor," where "the cost in human life due to murder, starvation, and disease and reduced fertility has been estimated at ten million. The French did not behave much better than the Belgians in their part of the

Congo: population loss was comparably huge."[4] Germany's genocidal treatment of the Herero population and suppression of the Maji Maji uprising were brutal and deadly. The Japanese murderously suppressed the Korean independence movement, while the Russians dealt mercilessly with the Poles and their rebellious subjects in the Caucasus and Central Asia.

America failed to live up to its constitutional value that all are created equal in its systematic displacement and destruction of its Native American population. Britain itself found it difficult to balance a vision of improvement and advancement with imperialism. Too often, its military power became the instrument to advance the spread and the maintenance of the empire. The concentration camps of the Boer War and the slaughter of Mahdist prisoners following the battle of Omdurman are only two examples of the inevitable human tragedies of imperialism. In addition, Britain's capitalistic imperialism distributed its benefits in an uneven manner even within its own population, primarily benefiting private investors and its elite classes. Certainly one lesson learned is that colonialism, even in Britain's case, has left us with enduring problems. The other lesson is that principled leadership, even in the case of colonialism, can also create lasting positive changes.

The Legitimacy of Values

In the previous examples, the British Empire failed to live up to the mission espoused by its liberal Victorian leaders. However, as Ferguson notes, these "Victorians had more elevated aspirations. They dreamt

---

4 Ibid., p. 249

not just of ruling the world, but of redeeming it. It was no longer enough for them to exploit other races; now the aim became to improve them."[5] While freeing slaves was the initial spark, it signaled a broader transformation of British policy, one guided by the principles of the Enlightenment and taken to the colonies by missionary societies for whom "spreading the word of God and thereby saving the souls of the benighted heathen was a new, not-for-profit rationale for expanding British influence." But saving souls was not sufficient. Britain also "aspired to export British culture."[6] This culture, combining humanitarian values, democracy, and capitalism, was Britain's greatest gift to its colonies. It was to be the defining mission of the century's most successful NGOs.[7] This values-based, non-profit-based form of colonialism gave the British Empire a moral legitimacy lacking in other colonial empires. It is this higher purpose and moral legitimacy that differentiates Britain from other colonizers. But this is only the first lesson from the British Empire.

End of an Empire and the Transfer of Values

It was the end of the British Empire in the twentieth century that ensured its positive and lasting legacy. Consider the alternatives to British Empire in 1940. As Ferguson states, "the most likely alternatives to British rule were Hirohito's Greater East Asia Co-Prosperity Sphere, Hitler's Thousand Year Reich, and Mussolini's New Rome. Nor could the threat posed by Stalin's Soviet Union be discounted, though until

5 Ibid., p. 116

6 Ibid., p. 122

7 Ibid., pp. 122-123

after the Second World War most of his energies were devoted to terror-izing his own subjects. It was the staggering cost of fighting these impe-rial rivals that ultimately ruined the British Empire. In other words, the Empire was dismantled not because it had oppressed subject people for centuries, but because it took up arms for just a few years against far more oppressive empires. **It did the right thing, regardless of the cost"** (emphasis added by the author).[8]

Further, while the cost of fighting these empires crushed the British economy, made the British Empire unaffordable, and resulted in its breakup following the Second World War, the way in which the breakup was achieved, in many important cases, allowed Britain to pass along "the structures of liberal capitalism" that were "successfully established in so many different economies around the world."[9] More important, Britain was able to seed its democratic political roots to many of its colonies, ensuring that its values endured. As Ferguson notes, "nearly every country with a population of at least a million that has emerged from the colonial era without succumbing to dictatorship is a former British colony. In short, what the British Empire proved is that empire is a form of international government that can work—and not just for the benefit of the ruling power. It sought to globalize not just an eco-nomic but a legal and ultimately a political system, too."[10] The world we live in today is more democratic, less poor, and less violent because Britain used its power to create a better world even at the cost of losing its empire. Coincidentally, Britain has also prospered, benefiting from

---

8 Ibid., p. 296

9 Ibid., p. 358

10 Ibid., p. 362

the more stable world it helped create. Even lost empires benefit if they do the right thing.

These are the lessons that Britain's most successful colony, America, should consider as it forges its own legacy.

The Basic Ingredients of Global Leadership

If Ferguson is right that America is the only power that can lead globally, and if, in fact, the United States is already playing that role by default, what can we learn from the British Empire's rise and fall? If Britain's success story in shaping a better world is to be emulated, what are the basic ingredients of global leadership? How does the United States change its status as "an empire in denial"[11] and lead in the development of a better, more secure world? Why should the United States play this global leadership role?

There are several basic ingredients to global leadership. These include, for example:

- Hard power, in the forms of a dominant military, a vital and growing population, and access to adequate natural resources and land

- Soft power, in the form of a strong, diverse, and growing economy coupled with an attractive culture and freedom of expression

- Having one's own house in order; for example, rule of law, government that represents its people, adequate governance of its

---

11 Ibid., p. 368

economy and finances, access to unbiased media and information, and stability in the ways in which leaders are changed

- An inclusive society, where all enjoy equal rights and opportunity regardless of personal beliefs, ethnic background, or social status

- A values-based common interest that is rooted in ethics, morality, fairness, and liberty and where these things are constitutionally guaranteed and supported by access to education and a social net that provides opportunity and certain protections for all citizens

- Willingness to sacrifice short-term hardship to realize long-term goals and objectives that promote lasting peace, progress, and broader distribution of its values and systems

The Differentiating Ingredient: Values

Certainly, colonial empires other than Britain have enjoyed some of the items detailed in the previous section at various times. However, the British Empire is unique in that it combined, to varying degrees, all of the above elements. And it is the commitment to values-based common interest that to this day guides Britain's approach to partnering with the world to sustain its vision. Decades after the breakup of its empire, Britain remains faithful to, in the words of former Prime Minister Tony Blair, "Justice not only to punish the guilty. But justice to bring those same values of democracy and freedom to people round the world … the starving, the wretched, the dispossessed, the ignorant, those living in want and squalor from the deserts of North Africa to the slums of Gaza, to the mountain ranges of Afghanistan: they too are our cause."[12]

---

12 Ibid., p. 365

We need look no further than Rwanda, Darfur, and Syria to see the need for justice imposed from without. On occasion, notably Kosovo, Kuwait, and Sierra Leone, partnerships have worked to reduce violence and injustice and establish order. America has been an active leader and partner in some of these effective interventions. These interventions do not always turn out as planned—Afghanistan being a prime example. And they can turn out badly, as they have in Iraq, when values are compromised in favor of political or economic self-interest. Having the military, economic, and political capabilities to lead are necessary but insufficient. In fact, it is the willingness to do the "right thing, regardless of the cost"[13] that differentiates the legitimate from the predatory. America's willingness to do the right thing with its hegemony regardless of the cost is unproven but sorely needed. And America would do well to learn from the lessons of the British Empire.

Values Require Balance

During the author's career in consulting, our firm often worked with large multinational employers in the construct of jobs, roles, and responsibilities. An essential factor in designing a job was the ability to describe a role in terms of both its technical and emotional competencies (for purposes of this discussion, competencies can be thought of as abilities and skills). At one point, our company was the world's largest employer of actuaries. These serious mathematicians had to pass rigorous examinations to acquire the designation of actuary; there was no questioning their technical prowess. However, not every actuary could combine these technical skills with the abilities needed to relate

13 Ibid.

to clients or manage colleagues. The interpersonal skills needed to perform these latter functions were equally important to successful client interactions. Those that could balance technical and emotional skills were the most successful and adaptive consultants. So it is with nations. If America is to lead in the creation of a better world, it will need to balance its hard (technical) skills with soft (emotional) competencies.

In his *Harvard Business Review* article, the psychologist Daniel Goleman described the five main emotional competencies that drive leadership performance: self-awareness, self-regulation, social skill, empathy, and motivation.[14] While Goleman intended these to apply to individuals, America would do well to consider these competencies as it assesses its leadership performance and future aspirations. If America believes that extending the most successful elements of our constitutional, democratic, and capitalistic system is the best way to promote global growth and sustain peace, then our national job description surely must balance our hard capabilities with soft principles; it is the former that provides the resources for us to act, but it is the latter that can provide legitimacy to these actions. We need to be aware of how our actions are perceived and how they affect others (self-awareness). We must always regulate our actions, being certain not to abuse our hard power (self-regulation). We must convince others through discussion rather than force wherever possible (social skill). We need to understand and be responsive to the legitimate needs of others even if that requires sacrifices on our part (empathy). Finally, we must always be willing to "do the right thing" even when it might not suit our own interests (motivation). America has not always been the best partner to those in peril (think Rwanda).

14 Daniel Goleman, "What Makes a Leader," *Harvard Business Review* (Jan. 2004)

It has not always participated in important international forums (think the International Criminal Court). We have failed on occasion to regulate our power (think Iraq). When we fail to balance the hard and the soft, we fail to live up to constitutional (and universal) ideals. This has to change before America can lead.

Global Leadership Requires Global Citizenship

The example of Britain is pertinent to determining America's global leadership role in the future. An explicit global role description that offers the best features of our constitutional, democratic, and capitalistic system, and balances hard and soft abilities in the distribution of this system is the best way to pull others to us rather than push them to conform. If you accept that we live in an increasingly global world, and that the United States is the only potential country with the combination of hard resources and soft competencies to lead, we should learn from history. America, like Britain, may not always enjoy its present level of hegemony. At this moment it is in position to influence the future. The challenge is to avoid the failings of British colonialism while learning from the successes of the distribution of the British system and its values. However, before this can be done, America must get its own house in order and demonstrate that it can be a moral and ethical leader. Americans may view themselves as exceptional, but this does not mean that others regard us in the same way. In fact, the concept of American exceptionalism may cloud our self-awareness of the impacts of our actions. Self-awareness and attention to the other emotional competencies are important if we are to be truly exceptional.

Global Citizen Patriotism Starts at Home

Before we can become global citizens, we, and our representatives, must first become better citizens in our own country. We need to understand what it means to be a citizen—not simply the rights of citizenship but the responsibilities, as well. And these citizen rights and responsibilities need to be cast in light of America's desired global role. Effective representative citizenship is the foundation for a new model of American leadership; one that brings its hegemony to the world in ways that are truly exceptional. It is time for leadership that leads by example rather than by coercion, seeks consensus, and leverages our advantages for the benefit of all rather than to gain advantage solely for the United States. For over two centuries, America has successfully built its economic, military, and cultural capabilities. It is now time to create the global citizen patriots and representatives who can ensure that America and the world benefits from our strength.

CHAPTER 3:
DESPERATELY SEEKING GLOBAL CITIZEN PATRIOTS

Overcoming the myths of America. Citizen responsibilities and
lessons from the dead.

Great Citizens Are Essential to Great Democracy

American citizens are increasingly "mad as hell" about the lack of
progress on virtually all major issues: labor and jobs, racial discrimi-
nation, immigration policy and citizenship, education, food, air, and

water protection, the balance between privacy and security, foreign aid and policy, the types and amounts of taxes and who pays, the roles and costs of government, and so on. Partisan groups seek to place the blame of this lack of progress on each other, the president, Democrats, Republicans, business, Congress, special interest groups and lobbyists, election financing rules, Political Action Committees, the Supreme Court, and just about any other group or institution. Who is to blame? If, in an effective democracy, citizens have the ultimate say, the only conclusion is that we ourselves are to blame. But where is it that we are failing? The vast majority of citizens observe the law and pay taxes, give freely of our time and money to support others, work productively, care for our families and friends, participate in the democratic process of voting (at least in presidential elections), and generally have faith in the American system of constitutional values, democracy, and capitalism. We are proud of our history. We feel that America is exceptional. So how can we be so dysfunctional?

This chapter argues that our definition of citizenship in America is incomplete and out of date. Reviews of the very principles of democracy, the rights and responsibilities of citizens, and the civic structures that enable good citizenship will allow us to consider how the definition of citizenship can be better crafted to enable positive change. For now, we will ignore the important topic of how citizens delegate certain responsibilities to their representatives, which is the subject of the following chapter.

Citizens Defined: Rights, Responsibilities, and Emotional Qualities

A *citizen* is a native or naturalized member of a country who enjoys the rights and protections of that country. In America, those rights (notably freedom of speech, voting rights, right to legal redress, and the right to personal property) are guaranteed in the Bill of Rights, which provides the foundation for the legal rights and privileges granted by the state to its people. In return, citizens are obligated to obey the laws of the land and to fulfill specified duties (notably tax payment, jury duty, and military service). If we view the aforementioned as citizenship's basic rights and responsibilities (let's call them the technical competencies of citizenship), can we ignore the moral and ethical qualities that serve as the emotional competencies of citizenship? For example, can we be apathetic voters, intolerant of others, and insensitive to the needs of the disadvantaged and still be high-performing citizens? None of this is at odds with our technical definition of citizen rights and responsibilities. But surely these behaviors are at odds with both the values of the Founding Fathers and liberal traditions.

In *What Is Citizenship?*, Derek Heater argues that "freedom, which, after all, is the very essence of liberalism, does not mean a free-for-all: it requires vital moral qualities in the citizen to prevent this abuse."[1] Heater bases his statement on the arguments advanced by the American academic Stephen Macedo, who identified these moral qualities as "tolerance, self-criticism, moderation, and a reasonable degree of engagement in the activities of citizenship."[2] Heater goes on to identify three

---

1 Derek Benjamin Heater, *What Is Citizenship* (Malden, MA, Polity, 1999) p. 32

2 Ibid.

qualities that are particularly important liberal virtues. "One is moderation…no fanaticism, no extremism—for these breed intolerance." A second virtue, toleration, requires that "citizenly virtue must therefore incorporate an attitude of live-and-let-live; it requires a cultivation of empathy. People as individuals or as groups are different, but they are all fellow citizens and should be respected as such." Finally, "what the virtues of liberalism expect is the amelioration or resolution of these differences, not by coercion, but by reasoned persuasion."[3] Heater's conclusion that "citizenly duties are civic qualities put into practice" is an excellent way to state the need for the integration of technical duties and emotional qualities if citizens are to "understand what their duties are and have a sense of moral obligation instilled in them to discharge these responsibilities."[4]

It is not apparent that Americans "understand and recognize what their duties are and have a sense of moral obligation instilled in them to discharge their responsibilities."[5] Moreover, do American civic structures (for example, education, religion, media, and other elements of civil society) adequately assist citizens in gaining this understanding and sense of moral obligation? Without this moral obligation to the overriding concept of liberal democracy, can we expect to overcome groups of uncompromising partisans who advocate a small group view versus that of broader society? Preventing the tyranny of the masses is desirable, but this should not be accomplished at the cost of a functioning liberal democracy. Informed debate and compromise are the essential

---

3 Ibid., p. 33

4 Ibid., p. 64

5 Ibid.

tools of effective and legitimate democracy. Destructive competition is the weapon of partisans who would sacrifice liberal democracy to their narrow interests. It seems clear that the present state of American politics has shifted to the point where partisan obstruction is blocking compromise-based progress. Only the active and principled engagement of citizens can restore balance to the American governance system. Yes, American citizens universally support the cause of freedom for all and democracy as the preferred vehicle to deliver freedom. Yes, we perform our basic duties most days. Yet we lack clarity on the stylistic and qualitative aspects of citizenship and systems that coach citizens to perform on behalf of all.

The ideals that should inform our approach to the emotional qualities that enable our democracy to function for all have not changed from those of the Founding Fathers. But they do require reinterpretation in light of the needs of modern society; for example, changing demographics, an increasingly services-driven economy, increased urbanization, the need for global solutions to security, economic, and environmental problems, and so on. Some suggest that we need to recapture our historical ways of doing things. In fact, this is not possible. We cannot go backward. We are different in our ethnicity, how we live, love, and work, and how we interact with each other. The world in which we live is different. And the future we face is uncertain but ever-changing. How we reinterpret the roles and responsibilities of citizens is foundational to progress.

This reinterpretation requires citizen involvement, discussion, and agreement at a higher level than at present. Absent this reinterpretation, coaching, and common accountability, citizens will remain too often mired in their own religious, racial, gender, or economic position biases. These biases are exacerbated by media and special interests that are, in the words of *New York Times* columnist David Brooks, "bombastic, hyperbolic, and imbalanced."[6] While Brooks was referring to the Republican Party in this case, examples of Democratic Party bias are also common. Every citizen's toolkit needs to include the emotional skills that promote universal freedom and democracy: empathy for all, willingness to objectively balance competing views, the ability to change long-held beliefs, willingness to compromise and try things in lieu of gridlock, and motivation to drive change through revisions to our representative process. These emotional competencies are the software that ensures that the hardware of citizenship (voting, community participation, military service, etc.) runs properly.

Better citizens are the essential platform for an improved liberal democracy whose house is in order; one that can be a model for other countries and a consensus world leader. In Chapter 1, the failure of citizens and their representatives were identified as the two essential failures that are causing us to be "mad as hell." We will only get liberal democratic representation when we act as liberal democratic citizens; citizens who base their actions on, as Brooks suggests, "conversation, calm deliberation, self-discipline, the capacity to listen to other points of view and balance valid but competing ideas and interests."[7] This transformation of our citizens is a long-term process. But it starts with agreement on the additional emotional requirements of citizenship and accountability to them. Enhancing these capabilities are significant challenges to

6 David Brooks, "The Republicans Incompetence Crisis," *The New York Times* (Oct. 13, 2015)

7 Ibid.

our education, media, and political systems—challenges that cannot be resolved overnight. However, we cannot wait. Citizen patriots need to spark change now.

Patriots Defined: Activists for a Higher Purpose

At a certain level, most Americans view themselves as patriots. They love their country, support its authority, and identify with its broad interests. Historically, Americans have also avoided the main pitfall of nationalism; that is, they have not blindly followed government policy. Through protest, elections, and civil conflict, citizens have shaped the direction of the country in ways that have advanced the status of those who may have been "created equal" but have not been able to enjoy equality. These changes have often come only after traumatic events have required leadership and inspiration from patriots acting in the common interest and committed to "doing the right thing." For example, Madison, Jefferson, Washington, Clara Barton, Abraham Lincoln, Susan B. Anthony, Franklin Roosevelt, and Martin Luther King have little in common in terms of their background, experience, and focus. Their common denominator was a passion for "doing the right thing whatever the cost" on one or more important moral, ethical, and human rights issues.[8] These leaders, and many others, were America's virtuous Victorians. They saw injustice and took action. In their willingness to take on established biases and effect change, they became some of our greatest citizen patriots.

8 Ferguson

America's greatest citizen patriots have an additional common denominator—they take up large-scale causes that move us closer to our liberal democratic ideals, or they correct failures in that regard. Causes are the vehicles to advance ideals, and they require the passion and dedication of patriots who can lead. It is hard to separate the civil rights movement from Martin Luther King, women's suffrage from Susan B. Anthony, or the emancipation of the slaves from Abraham Lincoln. While in retrospect the social and human rights changes they advocated seem to have been inevitable, they were far from obvious at the time. Their ability to create constituencies of citizens committed to the same ideals are prime examples of the definitions of a patriot; that is, someone who loves their country and supports its authority and interests but, at the same time, advocates change designed to attain a higher degree of liberal democracy. These patriot leaders did not accomplish this alone. All causes need patriot leaders, but the most successful causes require the active enthusiasm and support of masses of committed citizen patriots. Citizen patriots and citizen patriot leaders are the essential instruments of change.

Today, as a result of principled citizenship and patriotic passion, we enjoy "a more perfect union," improved government "by (all) the people," and a country that better provides "liberty and justice for all."[9] But, even for great leaders, this is not always easy. Lincoln did not initially fight the Civil War to free the slaves. However, he did, in time, recognize that the Civil War needed a higher purpose. He overcame his own biases and background and advocated for the Emancipation Proclamation. Similarly, contemporary Americans need to reconsider some of their

9 Constitution and Gettysburg Address

traditional biases and beliefs and subscribe to an even higher set of principles and ideals. Think of this higher purpose as an enhanced version, as opposed to a revision, of the ideals of the Founding Fathers—ideals that will require contemporary interpretations of societal goals and human responsibilities that could not have been anticipated by prior generations of leaders.

What are these enhanced ideals? Aren't we already exceptional? Why do we need to reconsider our ideals? Let's start by taking truth serum.

The Myths of America: Are We What We Say We Are?

Facts don't lie—America can do better in many ways. Whether you look at child poverty rates, the shrinking middle class, increasing concentrations of wealth and income, the cost of education and health care, deteriorating infrastructure or inability to address environmental, immigration, or other current issues, it seems apparent that there is considerable need for improvement. But the facts can be misrepresented. Certainly, part of this dysfunction is the result of crony capitalism that biases the work of our representatives in favor of narrow and special interests; complicated by media and information sources that are often more focused on driving ratings and advertising dollars than in balanced reporting. Yet many among us would agree with at least some of the following statements about America:

- There is opportunity for all.

- We are the greatest country.

- Our democracy should be a model for all countries.

- Our strength emanates from our values of fair play, individual responsibility, hard work, and our religious nature. We are in the right.

- Our form of capitalism has proven to be the best over time.

- Our Constitution of 1776 is the essential, immutable framework that guides us into the future.

- Free enterprise creates economic success, which makes us happier.

In fact, these are myths and half-truths perpetuated by special interests working toward personal or small group economic advantage and political influence rather than performing as citizen patriots to drive broad-based societal progress. These interests can be called out if we look at these myths objectively. Without this objectivity, we lack the self-awareness to motivate change.

Let's evaluate the above myths using the InterAction Council's Universal Declaration of Human Responsibilities as a sounding board.[10] A short, four-page document authored by a cross-section of global leaders, it provides a useful way to think about basic human responsibilities in the context of contemporary societal needs and trends. It "seeks to bring freedom and responsibility into balance and to promote a move from the freedom of indifference to the freedom of involvement." It is designed to reconcile "ideologies, beliefs, and political views that were deemed antagonistic in the past."[11] Viewed from an American perspective, the declaration provides an enhanced description of the responsibilities

10 InterAction Council, A Universal Declaration of Human Responsibilities (Sept. 1, 1997)

11 Ibid., p. 1

of citizens, not only to their own country but to people everywhere. Equally important, this declaration explicitly warns "that freedom without acceptance of responsibility can destroy the freedom itself, whereas when rights and responsibilities are balanced, then freedom is enhanced and a better world can be created."[12] Why are the responsibilities important to the citizens of the world's preeminent power? Why should we care? Let's come back to our myths.

The Universal Declaration of Human Responsibilities attempts to modernize and make explicit our human responsibilities to each other. It identifies five areas of responsibility: (1) Fundamental Principles for Humanity (for example, humane treatment, dignity, and self-esteem for all based on ethical standards); (2) Nonviolence and Respect for Life; (3) Justice and Solidarity; (4) Truthfulness and Tolerance; and, (5) Mutual Respect and Partnership. Do the myths of America stand the scrutiny of these well-articulated human values and responsibilities?

- **There is opportunity for all**: The declaration includes principles of justice that make "serious efforts to overcome poverty, malnutrition, ignorance and inequality." We live in a rich country, yet approximately 25% of our children are raised in poverty. Is this opportunity for all?

- **We are the greatest country**: The declaration states, "every person has a responsibility to respect life" and "to act in a peaceful, non-violent manner." Do we respect life when we allow the mass distribution of guns and gun death rates that are approximately

---

12 Ibid.

four times that of other developed countries? Can we be a great nation if we fail to make every effort to respect life?

- **Our democracy should be a model for other countries**: The declaration states that "the exclusive insistence on rights can result in conflict, division, and endless dispute, and the neglect of human responsibilities can lead to lawlessness and chaos." We have a Bill of Rights, but where is our Bill of Responsibilities? In addition, if our government is the structure that delivers democracy, why is it that America's ratings of government effectiveness have consistently declined since 1996[13] and that we compare unfavorably with Canada, the United Kingdom, Germany, and Sweden on overall ratings of the effectiveness of national government?[14]

- **Our strength emanates from our sense of fair play, individual responsibility, hard work, and our religious nature. We are in the right**: The declaration notes that "global problems demand global solutions, which can only be achieved through ideas, values, and norms respected by all cultures and societies." It seems fundamental that these ideas, values, and norms not be those of uncompromising fundamentalists, that our solutions not rely on misuse of our strong and professional military, and that individual citizens capably perform their responsibilities. We were not in the right in the second Iraq war or in our neglect of the Rwandan genocide. We are not in the right when we allow religious fundamentalists to block compromise and progress, and we are not in the right when we disenfranchise primarily minorities, the poor, and the young when we restrict voting rights.

---

13 Bok, p. 182

14 Ibid.

- **Our form of capitalism has proven to be the best over time:**
The declaration states, "wealth must be used responsibly in accordance with justice and the advancement of the human race." More and more, America's current form of crony capitalism provides the vast majority of our capitalistic gains to a shrinking percentage of Americans. At the same time, the increased risks associated with this crony capitalism fall on society in general rather than on those few who create the risk. Capitalism has proven its merit in relation to other economic models. But American capitalism in its current state often promotes neither justice nor advancement for all.

- **Our Constitution of 1776 is the essential, immutable framework that guides us into the future:** Jefferson and the Founding Fathers knew that their Constitution and Bill of Rights would need to adapt to changing mores and societal needs. In fact, we have amended our Constitution twenty-seven times (the first ten are known as the Bill of Rights). However, doesn't it seem odd that there have been no substantive amendments since 1971, nearly a half-century of unprecedented social, technological, economic, and political changes? For example, our inability to update election financing rules has given well-funded interests the ability to control who can run for Congress and president, their platforms, and the information that often distorts rather than balances candidates' positions.

- **Free enterprise creates economic success that makes us happier:** For Republicans and many Democrats, it is an act of faith that economic growth is the key to creating a happy electorate. Growth in GDP, increases in consumption, and unrestricted free enterprise are central tenets of that faith. But are policies to increase economic growth the same thing as policies to increase citizen well-being? Is this a false choice? Should our representatives be more focused on goals that researchers tell us actually do increase happiness?[15] For example, how to provide citizens with opportunities for improved education and personal development, meaningful work that contributes to society, improved support networks for families, the elderly, and the disabled, policies that support time with family and time to learn, explore, and travel, and programs that enhance security against crime, invasion of privacy, natural disasters, food or water shortages, environmental degradation, and so on? Balancing budgets is important over time. But let's balance our economic and social goals, as well. America is the greatest economic power. But we are far from the happiest society.

Most myths contain elements of truth. There are good reasons that people want to immigrate to America, attend our universities, and consume our products. The United States is a great country. However, improved self-awareness of our shortcomings is the first step to sustaining and progressing our ideals. Global citizen patriot leaders committed to doing the right things and committed followers willing to agitate peacefully in support of changes are the spark needed to ignite change.

---

15 Ibid.

Global Citizen Patriots: The New Elite

America's historical development was guided by a relatively small group of economically and educationally advantaged elites who were much influenced by the liberal democratic views of the Enlightenment. This elite-led version of America worked well as the country distributed its vast natural wealth to a fast-growing middle class for whom capitalistic economic progress and democratic values went hand in hand. To be sure, the economic elite selfishly distributed the fruit from large pieces of the economy (steel, railroads, mining, cotton, and land development were notable monopolies) while being inattentive and resistant to social policy issues. They allowed slavery to persist for far too long, failed to prevent the systematic displacement, marginalization, and murder of Native Americans, allowed women to remain disenfranchised until 1920, and failed to provide even basic securities and protections for the poor and waves of immigrants. Great capitalists are not necessarily great liberal Democrats. They enjoy the advantages of freedom and free enterprise but, with one exception, have little reason to balance their capitalism with social policy advancement.

That one exception—social unrest—has been a catalyst to address social injustices and advance liberal democracy. In the case of slavery, resolution required the Civil War. In the case of basic social protections, the unemployment, hunger, and poverty of the Depression years of the 1930s drove the remarkable social programs of the New Deal. In the case of garment and factory workers' wages and working conditions, it took agitation by the media to expose the problems and generate labor movements that, over time, have created much higher standards. Media exposure of racism and racial conflict helped create the civil rights movement. Pollution of our water, soil, and air resulted in protests, legal actions, and cleanup requirements by environmental activists that have remediated pollution and helped to sustain our natural resources. The capitalistic elite consistently fought these changes but in the end adapted (or went out of business). Today's social protections and safety nets in the United States are as strong as they have ever been, and our capitalist system is generating remarkable profits for both individuals and companies. The combined system of Constitution, capitalism, and democracy works. However, it is a system that requires regular rebalancing.

Today, we face a new and long list of challenges to the balance of our constitutional, capitalistic, and democratic system. All three elements have become problematic to varying degrees. Only by revisiting and clarifying our Constitutional ideals and rebalancing our capitalistic and democratic systems can we expect to advance our society, serve as a model for others, and create the policies and plans that will permit continuous improvement. A new group of leaders, committed to doing the right thing regardless of the cost, is needed to expose the myths and flaws in our system, propose changes to the critical areas of change that will drive the greatest improvements in that system, and create a constituency of voters who can force change. These new leaders need to think beyond economic, social, geographic, religious, ethnic, and other influences to refocus on universal human responsibilities. Let's debate the contemporary meanings of "all men are created equal," "for the people," and "by the people" (we don't need to change the words; rather, we need to better understand what they mean in a global, constantly changing world). And this debate should focus on changing the areas that are most responsible for dysfunction in the system; that is, uninformed and disengaged citizens, and corrupt and uncompromising representatives working for special interests.

In the past, it was citizen patriot leaders that created the movements that addressed specific social issues (creating jobs during the Depression, women's suffrage, etc.). At present, our issues are more complex and interrelated. Issues of inequality, racism, security, trade, environmental degradation, job creation, access to education, and citizen satisfaction are multidimensional and not easily addressed solely through passage of singular pieces of legislation. Rather, our constitutional, capitalistic, and democratic system can best be updated, and rebuilt where necessary, if we are anchored by a common platform understood by all; a platform that interprets constitutional values in a contemporary way and clearly defines universal human responsibilities. Much work has already been done in these areas (as evidenced in the earlier reference to the Universal Declaration of Human Responsibilities). Equally good work has been done by the United Nations and other groups in defining universal principles and rights and human development goals. Educational and media forums exist where these updated ideals, resultant responsibilities, and their implications can be debated and turned into well-reasoned and clearly communicated alternatives for the electorate to consider.

Forming a New Elite of Global Citizen Patriots

Central to the success of this effort is the emergence of new citizen elites who can lead this effort. The role description for the global citizen patriot leader would combine the technical competencies to discuss what to do and the emotional competencies to determine how to do it. Examples of the technical requirements are subject matter expertise, ability to articulate a fact-based position, strong critical thinking capability, a sense of both history and future trends, and a global perspective. These leaders need to be respected as experts. But they also need to demonstrate their commitment to ideals and demonstrate the emotional competencies that will allow their technical expertise to emerge as objectively as possible. These leadership traits include, for example, a willingness to see both sides of an argument, a willingness to alter a position (or compromise) when confronted with a compelling counterargument, the ability to discern and articulate the implications of their arguments on different groups, the courage to raise unpopular issues, and the ability to develop a consensus solution. With one exception, it is conceivable that the new elite could come from academia, business, the media, or any profession.

The important exception is that elected officials, or those who have stated that they wish to run for elected office, cannot be debate leaders. The separation of the debate process from the political process is critical to its credibility. If you believe that the current political process in the United States is hopelessly compromised by the impact of money and well-organized special interest groups, it seems logical to protect the citizen education and issue debate process from the political process. In his *The Discourses*, Machiavelli noted the inability of Athens to protect its democracy from "the arrogance of the upper class" and "the licentiousness of the general public." America's democracy, for its own sake and that of the world, needs to free itself from its traditional money-driven elite and from the referendum-based tyranny of the masses. By separating the process of informed debate on the issues (and resultant citizen education) from the political parties and the political process in general, we create the opportunity for reasoned debate. It is this ongoing, reasoned debate that will create informed global citizen patriots, one of the two essential reforms that will allow America to prevent its democracy from a fate similar to that of Athens. And, in the course of these debates, we will create a new elite—those concerned with the continued progress of our Founding Fathers' ideals and the changes that will facilitate that progress. Failure to create and support this new elite will limit us to the current political system of myth, bias, and special interest rule. The inability to overcome these failings has a cost. When geopolitical leaders and their citizens fail, people die or become refugees, economies fail, and environments deteriorate.

What's at Stake? Ask the Dead

There are few more moving experiences for Americans than visiting the Normandy American Cemetery and Memorial: 9,387 white headstones, perfectly laid out in pristine rows in beautifully landscaped grounds, recall the ultimate sacrifice made by so many Americans in World War II. As you walk among the headstones, you can read the names of each soldier, the unit that soldier fought with, home state, and the date of death—American citizens who gave their patriotic last full measure to help rid the world of Nazi tyranny. It is a place of unbearable sadness; not only for the lives lost, but also for the lost potential of the dead.

The author's Dad, a veteran of the Normandy campaign, wrote of his near-death wounding by a sniper. Second Lieutenant John M. Regan Jr. (22nd Infantry, 4th Army Division) was probably typical of

American small unit commanders. A Minnesotan from a middle-class, Depression-era family, he attended Yale on scholarship and graduated six months early to join the war effort. His fight lasted only four days from his unit's deployment in Normandy on June 18, 1944. As he describes in a subsequent letter to his parents, "we ran into considerable shelling by German 88's on the midday of the 22nd after a little skirmish in the morning. In the afternoon, we moved out to proceed north. It was then that we had to cross a couple of fields where they had good observation of us. Naturally they opened up with machine guns and other small arms and, boy, let me tell you, bullets were literally kicking up the ground at your feet… a second or two later one of their bullets clipped me," hitting "behind and below my right ear." What he did not share with his parents was the fact that even a centimeter difference in the placement of the shot could have ended his life. Second Lieutenant Regan's combat career was over. He spent the rest of the war "gold-bricking" first in an English hospital and then as a non-combat logistics officer traveling throughout liberated Europe.

Later in life, Dad would often reflect on all the blessings that life had bestowed on him: being born in America, fine parents, access to top flight education, great business opportunities (Dad became the CEO of Marsh & McLennan Companies and a director of several other Fortune 500 organizations), six "sensible" children and a loving wife, durable friendships, and a long and healthy life. As little as a centimeter difference on a single bullet allowed him to experience the joys of a fruitful and productive life. Wandering in the cemetery at Colleville-sur-Mer in Normandy, it is easy to find the markers of Minnesotans (and other states) of the 22nd Infantry, 4th Division. We cannot ask them about their futures and the opportunities that never existed for them. But we can surmise that none of them expected to permanently rest so far away from home. It is also reasonable to assume that these heroic patriots would have forgone their sacrifice if there had been a better way to defeat Nazism.

Historians reflecting on the rise of Hitler and Nazism note several junctures when the German people or the Allies could have intervened to prevent the rise of Hitler and Nazism. Perhaps this is the lesson the patriotic dead would share with us: engaged and informed citizenship matters. It is citizens who have the ultimate power to select leaders and hold them accountable to universal human rights and responsibilities. Patriotic sacrifices will be necessary at times. American security and happiness is increasingly tied to global security and happiness. Global citizen patriots, led by representatives who truly work in the interests of all, are our best opportunity to honor the patriotic dead by recognizing the costs of failed citizenship and representation.

So, in a way, we can ask the dead. We cannot give back the opportunities of life that they were prevented from enjoying. But we can learn from history—we can observe what has worked best and what has failed. Dad always felt he lived in a country remarkable for its freedoms, its principles, and its ability to change. Had he not survived his Normandy experience, he would have died knowing that he did his patriotic best to protect these values, both for Americans and for others. Defeating Nazism was worth the sacrifice of life. History suggests that more informed and activist German citizens should have acted to counter Hitler's rise to power. They failed to do so. It is our responsibility as global citizen patriots to proactively engage and act in support of basic human rights. This is the best way for principled, activist citizens and their leaders to minimize patriotic sacrifice. We owe this to the patriotic dead, ourselves, and future generations.

Great citizens led by a great representative elite is the only formula that can rebalance our system of democracy and capitalism. There is much to be done to overcome the myths of America. The system is dysfunctional. However, understanding how our democracy and capitalism is failing is the necessary first step in reform. This requires that we have reasonable clarity about what the system is for, which is the subject of the next chapter.

What is it that makes America unique? How do our values interact in a systematic way with our democracy and capitalism to create a better society? How do we adapt this system to the realities of seemingly ever-accelerating changes around us? How do citizens and their representatives play their roles in adapting our system to ensure its durability and relevance? Chapters 4 and 5 will begin to tackle these, and other, questions.

CHAPTER 4:
BALANCING CONSTITUTION, DEMOCRACY, AND CAPITALISM

Navigating to a more balanced system.

What's the System For?

If global citizen patriots and their representatives are the ultimate authority and vehicle for change, how do we arrange "our laws and institutions so as to best enable people's freedom to change?"[1] What limits do we impose on ourselves in the interest of creating a better society for all? Here again, it's about balance—between individual rights and responsibilities to collective society. These latter responsibilities create the need for both legal and self-imposed limits in many areas; for example, material and economic limits, social and traditional limits, and political limits. If a liberal democratic society requires that citizens not only be "free to choose, but that they also be able to choose well,"[2] then certainly Yuval Levin has it correct when he states, "a liberal society depends on the long way of moral formation." His concept of "the long way of moral formation"[3] focuses on broad-based societal advancement, as well as supportive institutions that facilitate citizens' ability to participate and be secure in this advancement. To Levin's way of thinking, this "moral formation" needs to be guided by "soul-forming institutions," including "flourishing family, rewarding work, a liberal education, or a humbling faith."[4]

Each of us is influenced in different ways by our families and friends, our religious beliefs, our education, and the types of work and leisure that we experience. These "soul-forming institutions" are incredibly varied. Indeed, this lack of uniformity promotes a broad and diverse society. On the other hand, it makes consensus on many issues very difficult. We might all agree on life, liberty, and the pursuit of happiness, but

---

1 Levin, First Things, p. 2

2 Ibid.

3 In an ever-changing world, a moving target that must balance traditional versus emerging values in all areas central to a well-functioning society. These areas include development of both human intellect and "habits of virtue." Ibid.

4 Ibid., p. 4

citizen rights and responsibilities, the ways in which we make decisions, and the economic principles that govern how we share resources and promote progress are all areas of historical disagreement. The lack of clarity as to how our constitutional, democratic, and capitalistic system might best work together to better serve citizens should be an ongoing and regular discussion. A holistic and strategic approach to updating the system is preferable to engaging in ongoing tactical disputes on matters such as taxation, budgets, deficits, size of government, and the like. These issues are secondary distractions to the central issue of how the overall system should be balanced for both its individual citizens and collective society. Constant focus on singular tactical issues plays into the hands of biased special interests. Only by examining changes in a system-wide (constitution, democracy, and capitalism) context can policy trade-offs be more clearly understood, thereby promoting more explicit choices and integrated solutions.

Our three-tiered system has evolved in many ways since the nation was founded. Some of these changes were planned and intentional, some reactive and impulsive, and, too often, the product of inadequate discussion or biased information. Periodically, it becomes evident that pieces of the system are painfully out of date. Like a biological entity, failures in one part of the system infect the broader whole. Periodic checkups and interventions are essential to good biological health. So it is with governing systems. One reason we are "mad as hell" is that the present system is clearly dysfunctional, and yet we seem unable to agree on a diagnosis or treatment plan.

Citizens need to ask themselves—are we serving the system rather than having it serve us? Each element of our constitutional, democratic, and capitalistic system plays an influential role on the whole. By reexamining the purpose of the overall system, and each component piece's role, we can hope to develop a clearer and better-integrated system of constitutional ideals, supportive democratic structures and processes, and capitalistic principles that stimulate economic growth, citizen opportunity, and societal progress. Better balance among these often-conflicting influences is also required if we are to take a long-term focus and be less susceptible to distracting and potentially destructive short-term thinking.

Our political parties have little interest in a review of the system. Entrenched special interests certainly abhor anything that might compromise their influence. A corrupt system works for them. Global citizen patriots, as the intended customers of the system, need to make their preferences clear and their directions firm. From a global perspective, when we fail to balance the elements of our system in ways that support our values, we give credibility to alternative forms of government that fail to share values of, for example, basic human rights, democratic choice, and economic opportunity for all. The ability to reaffirm and update what our system stands for has been a brilliant historical competency of the evolution of this country—a brilliance that is completely consistent with the principles of our founders and, at the same time, adaptable to the changing needs of its citizens and the world.

At present the twin support structures of American democracy and capitalism are failing to deliver needed adaptations. Democracy and capitalism are the supports that make our constitutional values become reality. But they cannot be adapted without proper steering. If the American Dream is to continue to evolve, prosper, and lead in the twenty-first century, it will be because global citizen patriots and their representatives are able to overcome special interests, reach compromise positions on disparate individual beliefs and preferences in the interests of collective progress, avoid serving special interests, and make the sacrifices needed to ensure collective progress. This evolution and progress is consistent with the vision of our founders and is the best way to honor the ultimate sacrifices made by the global citizen patriots resting in the American cemeteries in France, Belgium, Luxembourg, Italy, England, The Philippines, Arlington, Virginia, the Presidio of San Francisco, and thousands of other locations. We owe it to them that future sacrifices respect and extend the values that they fought for. Today's global citizen patriots are central to evolving those values to address contemporary issues and provide morally formed guidance for changes to our democratic and capitalistic support structures. We need to take the system back.

What is the system for? It is to preserve and evolve our historical values, ensure that sacrifices are not made in vain or unnecessarily, and provide increasing value to the customers of the system—its citizens. What should America preserve and adapt? This starts with questions of both values and value. And in our three-tiered system, these questions begin by examining the steering wheel of our society—constitutional values.

Values and Value

The unprecedented speed and scope of change demands that we periodically rethink what America stands for (our values) and what citizens want from the system (the things that we value). While we enjoy well-established, values-based constitutional and legal foundations, these are increasingly difficult to sustain in the face of globalized trade and commerce, technological advances that redefine and relocate work, proliferation of weapons of mass destruction, environmental degradation, changes to family, religious, and other traditional social structures, massive refugee movements from war-torn and insecure geographies, and privacy and security issues that need to be balanced with the benefits of continued information proliferation and access. Our constitutional values and supporting democratic and capitalistic structures cannot expect to adapt to such broad and global changes by relying solely on our history. However, we can use historical values to help guide our strategies to deal with the previously mentioned, and other, issues. Settling these issues of values, first and foremost, is the key to a twenty-first-century America that is morally formed by its traditional values and adapts those values to deserve the global leadership role that only it is capable of.

Constitutional Values: What Do We Stand For?

Followers of the 2015–2016 presidential debates might have noticed a pattern. Following uniform assertions that the United States is the greatest country in the world, the candidates then launched into a litany of their perspectives on what is wrong with America: the current president, the other candidates, the other party, big business, Wall Street, illegal immigrants, unfair Chinese trade and monetary policies, Russian aggression, religious fundamentalism, and so on. In the interest of attracting voters, reality is obscured or avoided. Tax cuts for all rely on unrealistic economic assumptions, more and better jobs are promised despite ever-increasing job obsolescence driven by technology, restoration of a strong middle class is held up, with no clue as to where these jobs will come from or how we will prepare the workforce of the future to fit these roles, fiscal responsibility without takeaways or compromises, free tuition without debt, large cuts to central government without impact on services to citizens, universal access to health care without discussion of affordability, border security walls paid for by others, and the list goes on. Promises and hyperbole trump frank discussions of problems and the difficult trade-offs needed to address the real problems. Maybe Secretary Clinton's experience in government will allow her to get things done despite a dysfunctional and partisan Congress. Perhaps the fact that Senators Rubio and Cruz are descendants of immigrants would have allowed them to combine sense and sensibility in addressing the issues of immigrants. Maybe Senator Sanders could fix Social Security, Medicare, and Medicaid without adding to the federal deficit. It is possible that either former CEO Fiorina's military saber rattling or Senator Paul's preference for reducing the overseas use of our military might be reasonable alternatives. You may even believe that Mr. Trump and Dr. Carson offer reasonable plans that can cut taxes and reduce the federal deficit. But when will we discuss the cons to all the pros that the candidates highlight?

Perhaps this shameless avoidance of truth and consequences is endemic to elections and politicians. Perhaps some of the blame can be placed on biased or inadequate media moderators. Regardless, it is citizen voters who will freely choose a candidate in November. But what allows us to choose well? What are the values that inform our choices on the pressing issues of the twenty-first century? How should our values add value to the lives of individuals and collective society?

It is time to rethink our debates. Let's talk first about values. There are important underlying differences in the ways the candidates view the responsibilities of citizenship, the roles of government, the extent of social protections, intergenerational responsibility, environmental protection, wealth distribution, America's global leadership role, and other matters that require values-based balance. As Harvard's Michael Sandel suggests, "the problem with our politics is not too much moral argument but too little. Our politics is overheated because it is mostly vacant, empty of moral and spiritual content. It fails to engage with questions that people care about."[5]

For over 200 years, citizens have enjoyed increasing freedoms as American democracy has evolved. At the same time, capitalism has proven the best way for Americans to sustain progress. Indeed, the combination of democratic freedoms and capitalism-based progress, coupled with our ability to adapt them (sometimes painfully) is something most Americans might see as the secret formula of success. During these two centuries, the constitutional vision and values espoused by the Founding Fathers have been our foundation for evolution. There is no compelling reason to shift this foundation; the core values of our founders are as pertinent today as they were in 1776. However, there is reason for concern when our citizens lose faith in their representatives to govern and these representatives seem unable to face the myths of America and offer honest discussion concerning the best ways to progress. It is even more disturbing when citizens disconnect from the responsibilities of citizenship; most notably, informed voting. A discussion of values is the first step.

---

5 Michael J. Sandal, *What Money Can't Buy: The Moral Limits of Markets* (New York, Farrar, Straus, and Giroux, 2012) p. 13

What do we stand for? "Life, liberty, and the pursuit of happiness" are aspirations that are never fully reached. "Of the people, by the people, and for the people" (Lincoln's "Gettysburg Address") remains an enduring vision of how we govern our democratic and capitalistic structures. These, and the other principles described in our Constitution and the Bill of Rights, are only the starting point. We learn new things, gain improved understanding, the environment around us changes, we are increasingly influenced and reliant on others outside our borders, and we ourselves change. We live in a dynamic world. How we collaborate with others, how we invest in the future, how we share the fruits of progress, how we protect those unable to protect themselves, how we include all in our vision are fundamental values issues.

Candidates offer varying positions about immigration, guns, taxes, social programs, use of the military, abortion, and same-sex marriage but "are confused about what liberty and progress really mean and require."[6] How and why we support proposed actions or impose limits on ourselves are values-based judgments that need to be understood and agreed upon (or at least we need to agree on what we disagree on and let voters decide) before resultant policies and plans can be put in place. We endlessly debate how to shape society without agreement on how best to shape our "human soul"[7] (what we believe in and stand for). Do we stand for basic human rights and the responsibilities that adhering to these entails? To what extent do our candidates agree or disagree with the values described in the Universal Declaration of Human Rights and the Universal Declaration of Human Responsibilities? Voters have

6 Levin, First Things, p. 1

7 Ibid., p. 2

a right and a responsibility to understand candidates' positions on these Universal Declarations. Debating positions on basic human rights and responsibilities is the best platform to define the values that will steer the evolution of our democracy and capitalism.

These consensus values are what we (and future adaptations to our Constitution and our democratic and capitalistic structures) need to stand for.

Values: The Need to Know Better

Understanding candidates' positions on issues of basic human rights and responsibilities is a necessary but insufficient level of information. Voters also need to understand the context and the consequences of their votes. The adage that Americans eventually do the right thing after exhausting all other possibilities is ill suited to a fast-changing and increasingly dangerous world. The nuances of how we take on basic human rights and responsibilities are how we demonstrate our values. We are what we do.

The historical ability of America to evolve its values is a great success story. Through the efforts and sacrifices of "morally formed" leaders and supportive global citizen patriots, the United States has adapted "all men are created equal" to gradually extend the values of "life, liberty, and the pursuit of happiness" to the previously excluded: women, immigrants, Native Americans, the poor, slaves, the uneducated, the unhealthy and disabled, those of non-Christian faiths, and others our democratic and/or economic structures failed to serve. Regardless of religion, political persuasion, location, social position, or education level, Americans universally accept the values of life, freedom, and the opportunity to construct meaningful and happy lives.

But these values need to be refined and adapted as society progresses. Social progress extends human rights to previously excluded groups; advances in science and technology require new ways of teaching, working, and thinking; and globalization suggests the need for more global rules, laws, and institutions. "Life, liberty, and the pursuit of happiness" cannot be a static concept in a changing world. Nor can it be a concept that only applies to Mr. Trump's seemingly narrow definition of "us" as opposed to "them." Our interpretations of the values that underlie "life, liberty, and the pursuit of happiness" will retain their currency and vitality only if we thoughtfully and periodically adapt them. The way in which we adapt them is central to how America defines it leadership role. For example, if we support the basic human principle that all lives matter, do we mean only American lives? Are we willing to stand up for the lives of non-Americans? Historically, we have done so when explicitly threatened or attacked (for example, the twentieth -century world wars, the 9/11 terror attacks, the Korean War). We have not always done so, or we have intervened only belatedly, or half-heartedly, when the threat is to "others" (Rwanda, the Balkan conflict, Somalia, Darfur). Do we acknowledge that these "others" are, in fact, our equals? Our actions, or inactions, matter to these "others." It is a great responsibility; one that global citizen patriots ignore at their own peril. Do our values only extend to our borders?

Our values are constantly threatened from both within and without. There are radical individuals and groups who do not share the liberal values of inclusion and equality. Racists, psychopathic dictators, fomenters of ethnic genocide, and radical jihadists are examples of those who would deny others basic human rights. Few would consider them either good or right (right-wing ideology being separate from the concept of being ethically right). These individuals and groups require educational, legal, and, occasionally, forcible interventions to ensure that they are not threats to the rights of others. Great conflicts have been fought to overcome these enemies of humanity. Too often, interventions have come belatedly (Rwanda), only after far too many unnecessary deaths have occurred. America and its global citizen patriots have often played a role in defending worldwide human rights that promote "life, liberty, and the pursuit of happiness."

However, as long as the root causes of radicalization and injustice exist, America will have to defend itself from those intending to destroy our system. How are we willing to use our power and influence to help those beyond our borders defend themselves against these same threats? To what extent are we willing to sacrifice American lives and money to lead the intellectual, economic, and physical fight against radicalization, even if there is not an immediate threat to our own country? These are important choices that will speak volumes about the evolution of American values in an increasingly global world. How each candidate will approach these is central to global citizen patriots' decision-making as we elect new leaders. These new leaders need to help define, and then stand for, the evolving values of their global citizen patriots.

Our more explicit discussion of values needs to go beyond issues of globalization and external threats. The evolution of our values also has important domestic implications to the ways in which our democracy and capitalism change. At a fundamental level, agreement on how to apply our values helps ensure that policy options are as durable as possible. Our democratic and capitalistic structures are best served when they promote medium-term and long-term stability and reliability. Indeed, our versions of democracy and capitalism perform best when we stick to principles that minimize partisanship, populism, and short-term fixes. Global citizen patriots need to debate and understand the values that serve as the foundation for policy changes. Clarity on these values-based issues is the best hope to transform nationalists into global patriots and partisans into citizens.

How America can best globalize its values raises important basic philosophical questions. For example:

- If we have the power to prevent or minimize Rwandan-type massacres, and we fail to do so, are we in conflict with our values, not to mention basic human values?

- What levels of cooperation, compromise, and sacrifice (for instance, economic agreements that benefit others at some cost to us, treaties and legal constraints that promote global stability but add no value domestically, or the number of military lives we are willing to risk to fight tyranny, respectively) are we willing to endure for the greater global good?

- What things need to be sacrificed in the short term to produce better long-term progress and stability?

- Which groups need assistance to progress, and which groups need to sacrifice to help provide for this progress?

- What are the basic requirements of productive citizenship, and what are the consequences of failure to meet these responsibilities?

- To what degree do Americans accept universal values as espoused in well-conceived works such as the Universal Declaration of Human Rights?

- To what extent, and in what manner, do Americans support universal responsibilities as suggested in the Universal Declaration of Human Responsibilities?

Perhaps the best way to think about questions like these is to take a future perspective.

In his university-level course, "Questions of Value," Professor Patrick Grim provides a useful overview of the philosophical origins of values and value.[8] Looking back at evils that were common practice in the past, such as slavery, Grim asks, "under what circumstances is it appropriate to say they should have known better? When society looks back on our views 50 years from now, what do you think they will find most appalling?" Should we "know better" when it comes to:

- Exclusionary racial, ethnic, and wealth distribution policies

- Wide variations in the amounts of per-student education funding

- Active and passive restrictions to full citizen participation (for example, voting)

- Failure to allocate sufficient resources to significantly reduce poverty, starvation, infant and maternal mortality, etc.

- Unequal access to health care

8 Patrick Grim, "Questions of Value" (The Great Courses, The Teaching Company, 2005)

- Inability to provide uniform security and rule of law for all

- Failure to provide adequate food, water, and clean air to all

Addressing these points and other issues involves citizen sacrifice in terms of money and lives. The burden will be disproportionate for certain citizens. How we address these questions gets to the roots of how we construct our values to better serve our domestic needs and those of the world. As Professor Grim states, the ability to "know better" requires that we, as individuals and as a society, be able to treat with suspicion moral concepts that "coincide all too well with our personal advantage."[9] Three examples of things we might mistrust include:

1. "We tend to regard obligations to those spatially close to us as of greater importance than obligations to those starving on the other side of the world" (or in other parts of our own country).

2. "We are quick to regard our own advantages as things we have earned and others' disadvantages as things they had coming."

3. "We accept a strong notion of rights, overriding the wrongness that can be done by people acting on those rights."[10]

On issues such as these, will we look back at a later time and know that "perhaps we, too, should have known better"? If we believe in the concept of free will and that our biomechanical makeup and environmental influences do not predetermine our behavior, then we cannot "abandon

---

9 Ibid., pp. 78-79

10 Ibid., p. 78

concepts of responsibility and choice that are at the core of our values."[11] Global citizen patriots, and their representatives, need to "know better."

Values are embedded in the past but need to also be forward looking. Adaptations to values create short-term winners and losers. Global citizen patriots get beyond short-term winners and losers to recognize that values promoting "the greatest good for the greatest number over the longest run"[12] benefit all. America has a long way to go in adapting its values to an ever-changing world. Questions of values, and the candidates' positions on them, are essential variables in election choice. Indeed, questions of values are the steering mechanisms that direct how our democratic and capitalistic structures should adapt. In which direction will America steer humanity? Let's debate these issues.

Value: What Do Citizens Want from the System?

Think about how the things we value have progressed over the past two centuries. Nineteenth-century Caucasian American citizens farmed and manufactured, lived in large families often in one place for their lifetimes, received elementary- and secondary-school levels of education, relied on local government and civil society to provide basic supports, and formed opinions based on limited print media sources and events in their own geography. The system generally worked for this majority; their lives improved in terms of having more and more of the things that they valued. These often included, for example, increased

---

11 Ibid., p. 91

12 David K. Batker and John de Graaf, *What's the Economy for Anyway?: Why It's Time to Stop Chasing Growth and Start Pursuing Happiness* (New York, Bloomsbury, 2011) p. 28

wealth, better housing, meaningful work and job opportunity, improved health and longer lives, access to education, strong family, religious, and local civil society emotional and financial supports, improved access to life-enhancing, entertaining, and enjoyable products and services, and local institutions that provided security, order, and public and private support systems (transportation, banking, parks, etc.).

Largely excluded from access to these items of value were populations such as slaves, Native Americans, non-Caucasian immigrant groups, the poor and uneducated, and, at least in terms of participation in the political process, women. Constitutional values were not applied to all, and the things of value created by its democratic and capitalistic structures were disproportionately distributed. A great Civil War, the advent of the Industrial Revolution, increased urbanization, and new waves of immigration allowed broader groups of Americans to improve their lives and better participate in the democratic and capitalistic system. Our values evolved, distributing the things that Americans valued to more of its citizens. And this distribution of value pulled waves of immigrants to the United States.

Values and the things we value continued to evolve in the twentieth and twenty-first centuries. For most Americans, satisfaction of basic biological and physiological needs (air, food, water, housing, etc.) are things we take as givens. Social and private programs (for example, Social Security, Medicare, Medicaid, health and other forms of insurance) and effective military, police, and safety (fire, FDA, EPA, etc.) resources provide enhanced health, financial, and physical security. Effective rule of law and enforcement provide protection for personal property and rights. Increased urbanization and access to tertiary education have helped reduce (but by no means have eliminated) social barriers such as race, wealth, social position, access to education, and information. In general, we are, as individuals, free to pursue the things that each of us finds most valuable as long as we do not violate the rights or freedoms of others. For some, this pursuit is economic: a big house, a nice car, lots of money. Others may place more value on meaningful work, advanced education, or contribution to something bigger than oneself. Professor Grim suggests a long list of "good things in a life."[13] Examples include fun, children, a long life, good health, fame, leisure and vacation time, adventure, knowledge, generosity, friendship and love, talent, respect, honesty, and the ever-elusive concept of happiness.

Over a lifetime, individuals prioritize things based on their own values. For each American, "life, liberty, and the pursuit of happiness" means having the liberty to pursue the things of value that allow them to live their individual definition of a life of happiness. But how about the things of value to society as a whole? What responsibilities do individuals have to constrain their individual priorities in order to promote the greatest good for the greatest number over the long run? How do we balance individual things of value with broader societal values? This is where values meet democracy and capitalism. It is the combination of these three that provide America's direction (what we stand for) and define the way we deliver the best possible balance of individual and collective rights and responsibilities. Certainly, values need to be the starting point. But the structures of our democratic and capitalistic systems are the supports on which our values rest. And like our values, these structures need to adapt. These adaptations are constant. However, they can

13 Grim, p. 29

be viewed in terms of what we expect them to contribute to our overall values while providing increased items of value to our citizens.

Many Americans believe that economic progress is the key to continued social progress. This seemed correct, at least until the last several decades. A growing economy delivered great gains to average incomes, quality of life, and personal security. In addition, significant new public and private investments resulted in infrastructure improvements (in particular to communication systems), expanded social programs, improved access to advanced education, and remarkable expansions of American businesses. In the latter case, American companies are leading the continued transition from an industrial-dominated economy to a more diversified industrial, consumer services, information, and financial-based economy.

This success continues, despite ever-increasing competition. In its March 31, 2015, update, PwC noted that fifty-three of the world's one hundred biggest companies in 2014 were American, an increase of eleven from only five years before.[14] Of these American companies in the top one hundred, it is also notable that many of the fastest growing between 2014 and 2015 represented a diverse set of industries (Apple, Actavis PLC, Berkshire Hathaway, Kinder Morgan, Facebook, The Walt Disney Co., Wells Fargo & Co., and Celgene Corp.).[15] During the six-year period of 2009 to 2015, the five global companies with the largest absolute increase in market capitalization were all American (Apple, Google, Berkshire Hathaway, Wells Fargo, and Microsoft). Nowhere

14 Global Top 100 Companies by Market Capitalization, pwc (March 31, 2015)

15 Ibid., slide 16

is the United States more dominant than in the important technology sector, where America has eight of the ten largest companies in 2015 measured by market capitalization.[16]

If the business of America is in fact business, our business-driven capitalistic economy remains globally competitive and growing in profitability despite the major economic shock of 2008. Investors in these (and many other) companies have been rewarded with good returns since 2008, and markets (particularly the financial sector) have adjusted to increased regulation and scrutiny. The most successful American multinational companies are smarter, more innovative, more productive, more globally dispersed, and more reputation dependent than ever before. Their ability to outperform global competitors over time demonstrates that American capitalism, as seen through the lens of its most brilliant creation, the multinational company, works from an economic perspective. But does this value translate to social progress and the things that American (and other) citizens value? Is economic progress alone sufficient for social progress? We see how US companies continue to lead the global economy. But how does the United States shape up in terms of social progress?

What do citizens want and expect from the system? How should democracy and capitalism better combine to provide individuals and society more of the things they value (and remain true to our values)? It's time to review what democracy and capitalism are for.

---

16 Ibid., slide 40

How Does Democracy Contribute to the
System? Why We Are Failing

Democracy is the way Americans regulate our freedom. The way we regulate our freedom is dependent on our values. Democracy defines how "of the people, for the people, and by the people" works. Or doesn't work. As the noted political scientist David Held states, political systems, be they democracy, monarchy, or aristocracy, are inherently unstable and ever-changing concepts.[17] The instability of democracy is nothing new. For example, Held cites the failure of Athens's democracy was due to "its inability to protect itself from the arrogance of the upper class and the licentiousness of the general public."[18] How the Athenian concepts of demos (people) and kratos (rule) mix together defines the range of democratic forms. Who are included as citizens, what are the conditions for entry, what is the nature of participation, and what are citizens' responsibilities? To what extent are citizens subject to rules, who rules, what jurisdictions apply, and who decides?

History demonstrates that pure rule of the people (examples include early Athens, anarchy, socialism, and communism) in forms other than democracy fails. Representative democracy has triumphed over the test of time. But democracy's forms and effectiveness vary considerably. So what is the mix of demos and kratos that exists today in America? How does this mix work to further our values and create value for both individual citizens and society? Where are we falling short, and what adaptations should we consider? As the form of our democracy evolves, doesn't this also require consideration of constitutional adaptations?

---

17 Held, p. 40

18 Ibid., p. 41

American democracy is a unique mix of constitutional aspirations and evolved practices. As a practical matter, American citizens delegate kratos (rule) to a combination of "rulers chosen by the ruled" and "rulers chosen by the representatives of the ruled." These rulers "should act in the interest of the ruled"[19] and be "backed by coercive power."[20] At the federal level, and putting aside the "coercive power" of the legal system, this manifests itself in individual citizen voting combined with a system of geographic electors (the Electoral College). The electing process works within an overall system of checks and balances that fragments ruling power between the president, the Congress, the states, and the judicial system. The concept of minority representative leadership requires that our representatives be "equipped with the necessary skill and expertise" to guide the "impulses, sentiments, and prejudices" of everyday citizens who in many cases lack the necessary "experience" and "knowledge" to rule.[21] Ideally, these representative rulers' key responsibility is "governing in the public interest" (this public interest is assumed to live up to the community's values while balancing the provision of things of value to individual citizens and society). Domination by the few (for instance, the rich and powerful) is supposed to be prevented "through the creation of accountable institutions" where "the central mechanism" is "the development of an active, informed, and involved citizenry."[22] This engaged citizenry "should enjoy equal rights and, accordingly, equal obligations in the specification of the political framework, which generates and limits the opportunities available to them: that is, they should be free and equal in the process of deliberation about the conditions of

---

19 Held, pp. 1-2

20 Ibid., p. 37

21 Ibid., p. 24

22 Held, p. 60

their own lives, and in the determination of these conditions, so long as they do not deploy this framework to negate the rights of others."[23] It is this "principle of autonomy"[24] that reinforces individual rights while obliging respect for the rights of others.

In Held's opinion, the principle of autonomy is where the essential balancing act of democracy occurs. It requires "the creation of a system of collective, reflective decision-making which allowed the engagement of citizens in the diverse forms of political affairs that significantly affect them."[25] Citing Robert Dahl, Held states that five requirements are needed for a system to be "fully democratic."[26] These critical concepts are, quoting Held:[27]

- Effective participation: Citizens must have adequate and equal opportunities to form their preferences, to place questions on the public agenda, and to express reasons for affirming one outcome rather than another

- Enlightened understanding: Citizens must enjoy ample and equal opportunities for discovering and affirming what choice in a matter before them would best serve their interests

- Voting equality at the decisive stage: Each citizen must be assured that his or her judgment will be counted as equal in weight to

---

23 Ibid., p. 264

24 Ibid., pp. 262-267

25 Ibid., p. 271

26 Ibid., p. 27

27 Ibid., p. 270

the judgments of other citizens at the decisive stage of collective decision-making

- Control of the agenda: The demos must have the opportunity to make decisions as to what matters are and are not to be decided by processes that meet the first three criteria

- Inclusiveness: The provision of the powers of citizenship to all mature persons with a legitimate stake in the polity (i.e., transients and visitors can be exempted)

It is hard to imagine a well-functioning democracy that disregards or weakens these decision-making requirements. Yet, large numbers of Americans fail to vote, fewer are politically active or well-informed, candidates seem more focused on positioning themselves in the polls than engaging in substantive discourse, and Democrats and Republicans stick to platforms that serve the needs of a small minority of self-interested, politically active, major financial contributors whose interests often conflict with collective solutions. These shortcomings are harmful to well-functioning democracy. But the potentially fatal damage comes from uniformed and disengaged eligible voters. Informed political activism is essential to democracy if it is to be trusted to elected representatives. Representative democracy ends when citizens fail to provide "free and reasoned assent."[28] Enlightened participation, enlightened understanding, voting equality at the decisive stage, control of the agenda, and inclusiveness are certainly our rights. But they are, perhaps more importantly, our responsibilities. Global citizen patriots need to

---

28 Ibid., p. 253

be held accountable to these responsibilities. At present, American citizens are not.

Democracy for Twenty-First-Century Citizens

The shortcomings of our current American democracy are not confined to what is discussed in the previous section. In addition, our over 200-year-old model of democracy is increasingly ill suited to serve the interests of modern society. Perhaps Held's greatest contribution in *Models of Democracy* is to carefully present the evolution of the historical forms of democracy and offer a more contemporary version attuned to ever-increasing globalization. In order to evolve democracy in a more global context, Held relies on the work of Claus Offe and Ulrich Preuss, which defines three ideal criteria that citizens need to be able to hurdle in order to attain a "rational" or "enlightened political will or judgment." These are the abilities to be: (1) fact regarding (as opposed to ignorant or doctrinaire); (2) future regarding (as opposed to myopic); and (3) other regarding (as opposed to selfish).[29] Perhaps many Americans would agree that, in general, our citizens' command of the facts, focus on the present versus the future, and excessive self-interest versus societal interest are less than ideal. This suggests that we need to consider a model where citizens and representatives are accountable to Held's five requirements of effective representative democracy. At the same time, citizens need to develop the three skills needed to attain the required "rational" and "enlightened political will or judgment."[30]

---

29 Ibid., p. 232

30 Ibid.

What can be done to:

- Motivate voter participation

- Stimulate "reasoned assent" of citizens[31]

- Provide for less biased deliberation of issues

- Improve media scrutiny of candidates' adherence to facts, ensure that candidates are elected and rewarded for results in the public interest (as opposed to results that favor special interests)

- And improve awareness that the "principle of autonomy requires entrenchment in regional and global networks as well as national and local polities"?[32]

Held offers evolved models of democracy that can improve the deliberative capabilities of citizens (Model IX: Deliberative Democracy),[33] enhance our democratic autonomy through improved equality of citizen rights and responsibilities that do not "negate the rights of others" (Model Xa: Democratic Autonomy),[34] and ensure that America participates in regional and global networks in ways that extend our values and add value outside of our borders (Model Xb: Cosmopolitan Democracy).[35] The changes suggested by the first two models, Deliberative Democracy and Democratic Autonomy, can be thought of as what America needs to do to improve its leadership of self. Only

---

31 Ibid., p. 254

32 Ibid., p. 308

33 Ibid., p. 253

34 Ibid., p. 282

35 Ibid., p. 308

when this is accomplished can we expect that America will be able to provide the leadership of others (so desperately needed by the world) inherent in Held's model of Cosmopolitan Democracy.[36] These are critical issues as we consider the evolution of America's democracy.

At present, American democracy is failing to live up to it values and provide value to all citizens. This shortcoming makes us less able to lead by example globally. Portions of this failure can be attributed to the hurdles of our democratic model to resist corruption and to adapt to a changing world. These hurdles can, and need to, be overcome. Held's models offer reasonable and detailed suggestions for the types of changes needed. However, it is hard to imagine a reasoned debate of the changes suggested by these models in today's partisan political environment. Political scientists like Held can feed a reasoned debate of changes to our democratic model. But their suggestions need to be heard and deliberated by adequately informed citizens and representatives working in the interest of the demos. A critical first step is for citizens to embrace both the rights and responsibilities of citizenship. Equally important, representatives must have their incentives and responsibilities restructured to ensure that they represent the full demos and resist powerful minority interests. Chapters 5, 6, and 7 suggest the essential short-term and long-term fixes required.

However, even with changes to citizen and representative requirements, our democratic model is only one part of the overall system. If our capitalistic economic system is in conflict with our democratic model or is a source of democratic dysfunction, it will surely detract from the overall

---

36 Ibid.

system's effectiveness. So we need to turn next to the third part of our system, capitalism.

How Does Capitalism Contribute to the System? Why We Are Failing

Capitalism is the way we create and distribute economic value (often referred to as various forms of capital) to our citizens. Think of it as the playbook that drives our economy. America's market-driven capitalism has served the country well over time. It has worked best when it has balanced both the ability to stimulate and create economic growth and offer all citizens the opportunity to share in this growth. At present, America has the highest GDP per capita of any of the major global powers. Our capitalism has delivered the goods. However, in recent years, the rates of increase in our GDP per capita have paled in comparison to other, newer versions of capitalism.

Are these new forms of capitalism (such as the Chinese state-dominated capitalism) superior, or are they simply expedient ways to close the wealth gap? Does the current form of US capitalism support and reinforce our democratic principles or subvert them? Is American capitalism the Republican Party version seen as "an economic form of Darwinian science…where the market, like nature, should dictate who wins and who loses"? Or does it more closely resemble the Democratic version who claim to "like the market but not so much that they trust it to make things work out equitably," not wanting "anyone to go home angry, so their economic policy offers everybody a party favor and a lollipop"?[37] Webber's views of Republican and Democratic capitalism are more than a little cynical (he certainly seems "mad as hell"), but surely he is correct when he states, "under the pressure of global competition and technological innovation, it makes perfect sense for our version of capitalism to evolve. It not only makes sense—it's essential. The problem isn't that our system isn't changing. It's that we can't have a conversation about how we want it to change in public straight on."[38]

Balancing Darwin and Lollipops

Is it possible that the choices offered by the two political parties are overly representative of minority extremists or well-funded special interests? Do we agree that capitalism should reinforce, support, and be subservient to democracy, and not the other way around? Do we agree that things of value to citizens are not simply increased wealth and income? At what levels of wealth or security do priorities change from increased consumption of goods and services to pursuits of meaning and happiness? What actually makes people better off, and what is capitalism's role in balancing the production of these items of value? While these questions relate to the economy, they are at the same time values-based questions that impact how we organize our democracy. Webber is certainly correct when he calls for debate. The context for a debate on economic policies is the overall system of values, democracy, and capitalism.

---

37 Alan M. Weber, "The Future of Capitalism," *USA Today* (March 15, 2010)

38 Ibid.

This is hardly new territory. In their signature treatise on capitalism, *The Commanding Heights*, Daniel Yergin and Joseph Stanislaw propose five tests that measure the validity of market economies.[39] These are:

1. The economy needs to deliver the goods (not just growth in the economy but also higher living standards, additional interesting and productive jobs, better products and services, etc.).

2. It needs to be fair in sharing success (for example, equity, fair play and opportunity, inclusion of the disenfranchised and the disadvantaged, and prevention of socially destabilizing concentrations of wealth and power).

3. It must have the ability to cope with demographic challenges (examples include the aging of the developed world, the mismatch of population growth and availability of jobs and opportunity in the developing world, and political conflict between the young and the old on the cost and distribution of entitlement programs).

4. Capitalism should secure rather than degrade our environment. How do we extend adequate protection to our air, water, soil, plant and animal life, the oceans, and other natural resources to all global economies? Who pays for the costs of protections and remediation, how do we mediate cross-border environmental disputes, and how do we further develop our understanding and agreement on human environmental impacts?

39 Daniel Yergin and Joseph Stanislaw, *The Commanding Heights: The Battle for the World Economy* (New York, Simon and Schuster, 2002), pp. 408-415

5. Our form of capitalism should be consistent with and support our national identity. How can we leverage the global economy for optimal growth, retain national values and our culture, and provide adequate security? Increased ethnic diversity, shifting religious identities, exposure to different cultures, changes to traditional family structures, exposure to volatile global financial risks, and fears associated with the proliferation of increasingly powerful weaponry in the hands of terrorists can be very threatening to national identity. Can a historically Caucasian, Western, Christian, elite-driven country adapt to these influences?

These points demonstrate the need to evaluate values, democracy, and capitalism as a system. As Harvard Professor Michael Sandel suggests, we need to accept the moral limits of markets.[40] "We need to ask whether there are some things that money should not buy."[41] In a world where everything is for sale, how can values or democracy survive? Further, if we really believe the adage that money can't buy happiness, we should treat with extreme suspicion promises that economic policies alone will "make America great" once again. And we should debate what we want the economy to do for us. How can it make us happy instead of just rich? Further, how can our capitalistic economy be best adapted to be consistent with our moral formation? As Professor Sandel stated, "Norms matter."[42] If the notion of the common good is a central value of a progressive society, then "the question of markets is really a question

---

40 Michael J. Sandel, *What Money Can't Buy: The Moral Limits of Markets* (New York, Farrar, Straus, and Giroux, 2012)

41 Ibid., p. 7

42 Ibid., p. 76

of how we want to live together. Do we want a society where everything is up for sale? Or are there certain moral and civic goods that markets do not honor and money cannot buy?"[43]

Increases in GDP per capita are desirable but insufficient. As Robert Kennedy noted in 1968, GDP "measures everything in short except that which makes life worthwhile."[44] What about the social relationships that enrich our lives, the volunteer work that sustains communities, the time spent exercising to maintain fitness and health, the work done improving your home, and sustaining fisheries and clean water supplies versus depleting them?[45] None of these activities contribute to increased GDP. But all can contribute to better lives. Equally misleading are many of the things that are measured by GDP: things that actually destroy lives and happiness. As Jonathan Rowe stated before Congress in 2008,[46] "any measure that portrays an increase in car crashes, cancer, marital breakdown, kinky mortgages, oil use, and gambling as evidence of advance— as the GDP does—simply because they occasion the expenditure of money, has a tenuous claim to being reality-based discourse." It's time for new measures that more broadly support **what the economy should be for—namely, citizens' well-being.**

Economic policies make a difference. No doubt some people are intrinsically happier than others. Market-based capitalism will always result in inequalities of income (and therefore power) and comparative prestige (since we tend to evaluate our progress too often on our comparative

---

43 Ibid., p. 204

44 De Graaf and Batker, p. 17

45 Ibid., pp. 20-21

46 Ibid., p. 22

position rather than our absolute progress). Polls that measure life satisfaction have frequently shown that Americans are less happy than our counterparts in other developed countries. Denmark and other Nordic countries are often the poster children of success in terms of citizen happiness. Even *Forbes* magazine (self-described as "the capitalist tool") has acknowledged common factors among the happiest countries: small gaps between the rich and poor, attention to work-life balance, short working hours, and, comparatively high taxes. However, the United States is not Denmark. We are in very different places in terms of racial, religious, social, cultural, and economic diversity, the range of social programs and protections, global leadership capabilities and responsibilities, geography, demographics, and levels of dependency on neighboring countries. America has been, and should continue to be, unique in many ways. Our values and form of democracy define what we value and how we organize ourselves to deliver that value. Ideally, our market-based capitalism should organize our capital resources in support of our values and democracy.

What's the economy for? At the highest level, it exists to support our values and "life, liberty, and the pursuit of happiness." But at the individual citizen's level, the economy exists to organize our resources to serve the interests of both individuals and the community. Balancing these resources to create economic growth and enhanced quality of life is the essence of economic policies—policies that need to continuously adapt to changing circumstances. As John de Graaf and David Batker suggest in *What's the Economy For, Anyway?*, the economy should provide "the greatest good for the greatest number over the longest run."[47] Darwin needs lollipops, too.

The Misguided Market Society

In a June 2013 TED Talk, Professor Sandel stated that the United States has moved from a **market economy to a market society,** where life is overly dependent on how much money one has. Those with lots of money are able to evade mainstream society and not participate in the lives (and issues) of the majority who cannot isolate themselves. Sandel's examples of this include access to education, access to justice, and access to political influence (see Sandel's TED Talk of June 2013). Worse, as Professor Peter Rodriguez notes in his course "Why Economies Rise or Fall": "corruption goes along with increased inequality in income levels. Once you're in the system and have a little bit of money, it's easier to perpetuate your wealth and more difficult for others to get in."[48]

Market economies have to go beyond money if they are to avoid becoming corrupt market societies. Quoting De Graaf and Batker, economies rely on five types of capital resources:[49]

1. *Built capital.* The physical infrastructure humans create from natural resources, including the technologies, machines, and other products that comprise the economy.

---

47 Ibid., p. 28

48 Peter Rodriguez, *Why Economies Rise and Fall* (The Great Courses, The Teaching Company, 2010) p. 50

49 De Graaf and Batker, p. 48

2. *Financial capital.* Paper and electronic money and other representations of monetary value, including stocks, bonds, retirement funds, and so on. These assets are all dependent on trust, and their value is realized when exchanged for real goods and services.

3. *Natural capital.* Native plants and animals, topography, geology, nutrient and water flows, energy, and natural process that nature provides. All built capital is created out of natural capital.

4. *Human capital.* A person's body, skills, knowledge, education, and such interpersonal skills as listening, cooperating, and communication.

5. *Social capital.* The social organizations, laws, informal networks, markets, relationships, and trust that constructively enable people to live and work together.

Successful capitalist market economies need to orchestrate, in as fair and transparent a manner as possible, these capital resources on behalf of all citizens. At the same time, citizens need the freedom to take advantage of these resources as their abilities and level of motivation dictate. It is the government's role to impose rules and controls on these capital assets to ensure that they are distributed in a manner consistent with our values and democratic principles.

Examples of Capital Asset Mismanagement

How are we doing? Is our economy delivering the greatest good for the greatest number over the longest run? De Graaf and Batker dedicate much of *What's the Economy For, Anyway?* to documenting the failure of the American economy to invest and equitably distribute the five capitals. Egregious examples of how our market society is failing include:

- Deterioration of public infrastructure, including roadways, bridges, clean water delivery systems coupled with too little investment in efficient, high-speed public transportation alternatives, new parks and recreation facilities, and the other items necessary to both the routine maintenance and improvement of public assets. This failure results in reduced numbers of construction, architectural, engineering, administrative, financial, and other jobs that are needed to sustain a robust economy. Failure to adequately invest in infrastructure makes it harder to live, do business, and create and maintain productive jobs. Where is the twenty-first-century and market-based version of the Works Projects Administration?

- Short-term water, soil, plant, animal, and other natural resource management policies that reward consumption over sustainability and fail to recognize the remediation costs of pollution in the cost of the product. When we burn fossil fuels, we pollute the air, but the cost of these fuels to consumers does not adequately include either the current or future costs associated with remediating carbon released into the atmosphere. The eventual costs of reducing or eliminating chemical runoffs from industry and farms are not adequately reflected in the cost of products. Our unwillingness to recognize and include the full costs of doing business makes many of our current carbon-based fuels slightly cheaper today at a potentially great cost to future consumers. Rather than cheap gas, oil drilling subsidies, and further exploitation of public lands by the carbon industry, shouldn't we increase financial and other incentives to create a job-rich clean energy industry coupled with enhanced efficiency and conservation by consumers and energy producers? How can we alter the current incentives to promote sustainability and create new jobs? Where is the twenty-first-century and market-based version of the Civilian Conservation Corps?

- The inability to provide a universal system of both health care and incentives to be healthy is a national disgrace and an incredible waste of potentially productive capital. At 18% of GDP, our health-care expenditures are two to three times the cost of systems of other developed countries, with worse overall health outcomes, while subjecting citizens to dizzying amounts of plan alternatives, complexity, and interference in the doctor/patient relationship. This is certainly an unproductive use of money. The system can be better, faster, and cheaper when citizens insist on and accept a universal single-payer system where primary care physicians and health advocates orchestrate specialists, nutritionists, fitness providers, elder care, and mental health resources in a coordinated manner. Our primary care physicians need to be restored to the positions of prominence and control of the system that they enjoyed decades ago. The current system is owned by high-priced specialists, administrators, insurers, lawyers, and their lobbyists—much of this capital is unproductive in terms of both costs and health outcomes. Let's put family doctors back in charge, arm them with great customer service assistants, the best possible information systems and continuing education programs, and recognize their lead role with increased compensation based on their ability to create ever-improving and increasingly efficient health outcomes for their patients. In the process, we can create millions of new rewarding and productive jobs that focus on patient care while reducing the number of less productive and less rewarding claim processing, call center, and office and hospital administration jobs that offer limited career opportunity and are easily outsourced. Where is the twenty-first-century version of Marcus Welby, M.D., who cares about and cares for the overall well-being of his (or her) patients?

- Failure of our politicians, businesses, and citizens to balance the retirement income needs of society with adequate funding. Americans have been promised Social Security income, disability income, and Medicare, but inadequate monies are set aside to fund these long-term liabilities. This simply defers taxation to future generations or results in unfulfilled promises to the aged, or both. This is a basic arithmetic test that politicians and citizens are reluctant to confront. Honesty is the best policy: additional taxes (or citizen givebacks such as deferred retirement dates) are required. Nowhere is this a greater problem than at the state level, where unions and politicians have conspired to promise future benefits to state employees that cannot be delivered at present levels of funding. These liabilities are a great threat to public finance; a problem that only gets worse as it is deferred. As we face the limitations of public retirement plans and the unfairness of increased taxation of future generations to make good on these ill-advised promises, it is time to create a new retirement income system that ensures that all citizens have an actuarially funded public pension (Social Security) adequate to basic needs, complemented by tax-effective individual retirement savings plans that are funded by mandatory minimum contributions by individuals and employers. Real projections of the amounts needed in retirement and individual plans that will deliver the desired income at retirement are essential. These are not easy calculations. All citizens need to understand the mathematics of retirement income funding and investing. The foundations for this understanding should be delivered through the education system. But every citizen should have the benefit of access to an unbiased, highly skilled financial advisor who can prepare, monitor, and adjust each citizen's retirement income plan. Trusted financial advisors who receive the same vendor-based compensation regardless of where the monies are invested are fundamental to reforming the current predatory investment advisor/broker charade where the advisor's compensation and the customer's best interests are often misaligned. Where is the twenty-first-century version of the objective, third-party actuary who commits to a high degree of professional excellence and objectivity and works with individuals to meet their retirement goals? Let's re-create, enlarge, and fairly compensate the retirement advisory function in ways that professionalize the advisory business and protect its customers. At the same time, improved citizen awareness will reduce the ability of predatory financial "advisors" to prey on the uninformed and ill advised. An effective national retirement policy will ensure that each generation pays it fair share of retirement liabilities while overseeing that all citizens have adequate retirement funds.

- Inadequate retirement planning and funding is only one example of our tendency to outspend our income. At the national, state,

and local levels, gross public debt exceeds $22 trillion (www.
usgovernmentspending.com/classic) or 74% of GDP. As the costs
of inadequately funded entitlements rise in the future, debt levels are projected to exceed 100% of GDP by 2039 (census.com,
7/10/2015), levels not seen since the end of World War II. There
is nothing wrong with using debt to stimulate the economy as
needed. But there is a lot wrong with having no plan to manage
debt down when economic times so permit. Too often, when the
economy has produced annual surpluses, politicians have chosen
to provide additional tax breaks or give away additional entitlements that are difficult or impossible to alter when the economy
deteriorates. The inability to manage debt to acceptable levels simply passes the problem along to future generations. Treating the
problem with a combination of well-reasoned cuts in expenses
and tax increases will allow us to begin the debt reduction process and, at the same time, increase investments in education and
productive and rewarding jobs. It is not too late to put our financial house in order, but we need to begin now. Restraint of debt
should also extend to individual Americans. When we take on
mortgages and credit card debt, we enrich the financial industry
and place our financial security at risk. There is little doubt that
the financial services industry has made huge profits on citizens'
debt. Relaxed government regulation and tax-favored treatment
of mortgages, in particular, are indicative of the influence of the
financial services lobby in Washington, DC. Let's place limits on
the amount of aggregate credit card debt consumers can take,
reduce the punitive interest rates on credit card debt, and phase
out the tax deductibility of large mortgages (do we really want citizens subsidizing jumbo mortgages on millionaire properties?).

The ability to better live within our means will eventually free up money for more socially appropriate and productive uses, such as education, retirement savings, and consumer goods. This will have a detrimental effect on the grossly oversized financial industry and the large compensation packages of Wall Street employees. However, in the long run, a financial services industry that is based on trust and social contributions will help ensure that the market economy does not become a market society.

- We live in a world where refugee numbers have reached destabilizing levels as evidenced by the surge of refugees to the EU. How can we take on these problems and enhance the social capital that allows citizens everywhere to live and work together while at the same time demonstrating principled leadership as a country? One has to admire the Germans. First, they took on responsibility for the costs and liabilities associated with the integration of East Germany. More recently, they decided to take up to a million refugees, primarily from Africa and the Middle East. In contrast, US politicians talk about building border walls, increasing immigrant screening, deporting millions of non-citizens, and banning Syrian refugees altogether while justifying their positions based on fear of terrorism, competition for scarce jobs, and worries that a path to citizenship for illegal immigrants will distort the electorate. Why is Germany seemingly fearless, while the United States is scared? Maybe it is not just a matter of Germany seizing the high moral ground. What if they are actually doing this for a reason? The German population is aging, and birth rates are insufficient to maintain the needed workforce over time. Where will new generations of younger workers come from; those needed to support the tax base necessary to sustain the aged? Where will the large numbers of electrical engineers needed to replace and supplement a generation of retiring skilled workers come from? Taking in a million predominantly young refugees and integrating them into the German education system and its economy is the solution to Germany's demographic problem and a key to investing in the human capital needed to maintain economic growth. More important, it is the right thing to do from a values perspective. Rather than pushing human capital away with walls and restrictions and limitations on foreign students, wouldn't we be better off pulling families of young and motivated immigrants and the most talented students to the United States? America owes much of its success to its ability to integrate waves of immigrants into our society and economy. If demographics are destiny, we will need immigrants to rebalance our aging demographics and ensure that our economy has the human capital it needs to grow. Well-planned immigration policy is sensible market economics, good social policy, and a reaffirmation of America's inclusive values.

The preceding examples are representative of our failures to effectively manage and build the five capitals in total. Our oversized and predatory financial sector and resultant wealth inequalities divert resources that can be better used to sustain our natural capital, maintain and create built capital, develop human capital, and invest in social capital. In a market society where everything is seemingly for sale, it is inevitable that we will leave our values and our democracy behind.

Time to Rebalance: Boiling the Ocean

Skilled financial advisors and knowledgeable investors understand the need to periodically rebalance their asset portfolios to maximize long-term returns while minimizing risk. So it is with America's portfolio of values, democracy, and capitalism. When we fail to update our values to a changing world, our children will eventually come to wonder what we were thinking. When our representative democracy fails to govern, we abdicate our governance to socially destructive special interests, the judicial system, and short-term thinking. When we allow our market-based capitalism to create a market society, we concentrate power in the hands of too few and create social inequities that will, in the long run, certainly destroy social stability. Most of all, we the people fail to meet our responsibilities as global citizen patriots.

It's time to rebalance our portfolio of values, democracy, and capitalism, in that order of priority. This is an unbearably complex undertaking (or perhaps we would have already done it) that is every bit as complicated as understanding a human biological system. A former colleague used to describe overly complex tasks as trying to boil the ocean. What are the things that we can do to better understand and rebalance the system so that we can deliver the greatest good for the greatest number over the longest run? We can't boil the ocean (and even if we could, it would be a very bad idea). But we can take two concrete steps to ensure that our rebalancing efforts are directed by informed citizen values and are delivered by representatives who can effectively manage the tools of democracy on citizens' behalf.

The essential first step is to ensure that the experts that represent us are the most highly qualified executives that we can identify. On our behalf, these executives need to be able to manage the complexities of our system, advocate the changes needed to periodically rebalance that system, and lead the change processes. At the present time, our representatives are unable to perform these duties due to the perverse monetary and other incentives that negatively influence their ability to work for all citizens. Step one is to alter these incentives to ensure that our representatives are leaders, not lackeys to special interests. This first step is necessary, but ultimately insufficient. Elected representatives will only be as good as the citizens who elect them. Let's initiate a process that will create global citizen patriots who are able to understand and critically think about the issues and are subject to a citizens' Bill of Responsibilities. The longer-term process will be to cultivate citizens who take patriotic responsibility seriously and do so with an informed perspective that balances local, regional, and global needs—the global citizen patriots who will insist on change and ensure that representatives are accountable.

These steps are the subjects of the following two chapters.

CHAPTER 5:
ENSURING LEADERS, NOT LACKEYS

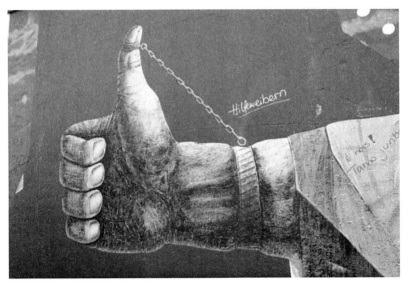

Why our representatives are lackeys—and how to free them.

Representative Government Is Only as Good as Its Representatives

Representative democracy requires, first and foremost, skilled and unbiased representatives able to balance the needs of their constituents with those of all Americans. It is their job to represent our values and lead the never-ending evolution and adaptation of our democratic and capitalistic institutions. This chapter will summarize how our representatives have been corrupted and suggest specific changes that will allow citizens to elect the best possible candidates, ensure that they are refocused on performing clearly defined roles and responsibilities, and provide them with the proper incentives and accountabilities to perform as we expect. Representative leaders are critical to the evolution of our system. They are our chief executive officers and, as a group, need to fairly represent and be held accountable to all the stakeholders in our system. Improper incentives and the ability of special interests to corrupt the elective and legislative processes have eroded the abilities of our representatives to lead. Too often, representatives charged with leading are instead lackeys to special interest groups. Global citizen patriots have to play a key role in these reforms, but we need to agree on the nature of the problem and the best ways to attack it. These are the subjects of this chapter.

How American Representative Democracy Is Corrupt

The evidence is overwhelming. Money drives all of the important steps of America's national elective process, controlling who can win, candidate positions on the issues, representatives' behavior once in office, their chances of reelection, and their future career and financial opportunities. Throughout their political careers, our representatives' positions are dependent on money. As Lawrence Lessig states in the aptly titled *Republic, Lost*, "we have a gaggle of good souls who have become dependent in a way that weakens our democracy, and we have a nation of good souls who see that dependency and assume the worst."[1] The dependence on money ensures that our representatives, regardless of

---

1 Lawrence Lessig, *Republic, Lost: How Money Corrupts Congress—and a Plan to Stop It* (New York, Twelve, 2011) p. 39

the state of their souls, are legally corrupted by the sources of those funds. Equally important, the seemingly predetermining factor of money impacts citizens' confidence in the system and their willingness to engage and participate in the elective process. As citizens' confidence in the process erodes, they pay less attention to the issues and fail to vote. The failure of citizens to vote allows smaller groups of committed voters to bias representative focus and performance in ways that over-weight their influence. Over time, this creates an increasingly radical-ized set of representatives less amenable to the compromises necessary to effective democracy. Consider some of the most egregious markers of representative corruption:

- Government subsidies and trade restrictions that result in much higher prices for milk (+26%), butter (+100%), cheese, shrimp, cotton, bananas, lumber, steel, and peanuts. Who do these subsi-dies protect? Not small farmers or startup businesses; in fact, the lion's share of these benefits are received by the largest farmers and Fortune 500 companies, arguably those who are least likely to need them to stimulate their economic performance.[2] Who is disadvantaged? The poor, who are less able to afford the higher prices, and low-cost providers (many of them in developing countries), who are unable to sell their products in our non-com-petitive market.

- Sugar costs that are two to three times more expensive than in other countries. This provides the top US sugar producers $1 billion in extra profits per year. Who is hurt by this protection-ism? Other American food businesses and consumers (every

2 Ibid., pp. 45-47

penny in increased sugar prices costs an estimated $250 million in increased food costs), American jobs (estimated at over 10,000 jobs between 1997 and 2002), and developing nations (to whom the negative impact has been estimated to be at least $800 million per year).[3] Why does this protectionism endure in the face of this evidence? Perhaps the large increases in campaign contributions by the sugar industry (approaching $6 million in 2010) are decisive.[4]

- Corn subsidies that, among other bad effects, stimulate the production of ethanol, "perhaps the dumbest 'green' energy program ever launched by the government" in that it is neither a good nor green fuel.[5] Corn and other biofuel subsidies were estimated to cost the economy more than $100 billion from 2005 to 2010. Why would Congress do this? Is there a relationship between the fact that presidential campaigns begin in Iowa, and that corn industry campaign spending grew to approximately $18 million in 2010? Why else would representatives support what Steven Rattner has called "The Great Corn Con"?[6] Corn policy increases consumer prices, requires $6 billion in annual government subsidies, makes cheaper foreign ethanol producers uncompetitive, produces dubious environmental benefits, and reduces food supplies to a hungry world.[7] Dumb, certainly. But also a perfect storm of misplaced values, poorly functioning democracy, and bad economics.

---

3 Ibid., p. 48

4 Ibid., p. 51

5 Ibid., p. 50

6 Steven Rattner, "The Great Corn Con," *The New York Times* (June 24, 2011)

7 Ibid.

- Fossil fuel energy costs that fail to include the costs of negative externalities, specifically, the costs associated with increased health care costs and the need to clean up this pollution at some point in the future. Just the $100 billion per year estimated impact of pollution on public health is staggering. So why don't our representatives do something about this? After all, pro-carbon reformers spent $22.4 million in lobbying and campaign contributions in 2009 in support of reform. The bad news for these reformers was that the anti-reform movement spent $210.6 million in the same time period. Is it any wonder that Congress failed to enact cap-and-trade emission controls?[8]

- *NY Times* columnist Nicholas Kristof nicely summarized the pharmaceutical industry's lobbying efforts in his February 18, 2016, column, stating "it spent $272,000 in campaign donations per member of Congress" in 2015 designed "to bar the government from bargaining drug prices in Medicare. That amounts to a $50 billion annual gift to pharmaceutical companies." Ever wonder why prescription drug prices are higher in the United States? Why does insulin cost six times more in the United States than in Europe for the same product? Even more insidious is the influence of pharmaceutical industry marketing practices on the utilization of prescription drugs. Isn't something wrong when the US population, 5% to the world's total, accounts for 80% of the world's opiates use? High prices and high utilization are not just a cost problem. The public health issue of addiction is a significant social issue.

8 Lessig, pp. 56-59

- The preceding examples of monetary corruption pale by comparison to the excesses of the financial services industry. "From 1999 to 2008, the financial sector expended $2.7 billion in reported federal lobbying expenses; individuals and political action committees in the sector made more than $1 billion in campaign contributions."[9] From the industry's perspective, this was money well spent. By 2008, 90% of financial investments traded in the market were exempted from the regulations that had remained in effect since the New Deal. The resulting proliferation of unregulated and opaque derivatives, for example, became a trigger for the 2008 financial crisis. But the ability of the financial sector to take increasing risk was not the worst feature of the influence of the financial sector in Washington. Rather, the government's implicit promise to bail out those financial institutions deemed too big to fail amounts to a $34 billion annual subsidy that in effect allows the sector to gamble with the awareness that the losses will be guaranteed by the government. As the economist Paul Krugman stated, "socializing the losses while privatizing the gains" benefits the privileged while taxing the rest of us to make good the losses.[10] Rather than jail terms, the largest Wall Street firms "earned $140 billion in 2009, the highest number on record"[11] at a time when most Americans were suffering the impact of a severe economic downturn largely caused by the excessive risk taking and the bad mortgage bets of the financial sector. It's enough to make you "mad as hell."

---

9 Ibid., p. 83

10 Ibid., p. 187

11 Ibid.

- Even lobbyists involved in the breathtaking exchanges of money for influence are shocked by the effectiveness of their work. When a tax code proposal was floated in 2007 to close a loophole that allows hedge and equity fund managers to pay a 15% capital gains tax rate on their income rather than the normal 35% rate, a huge year over year increase in both lobbying monies and campaign contributions (from $4 million to $20 million and from $11 million to nearly $20 million, respectively) had the desired effect of blocking the proposal. The favorable tax and regulatory treatment of these funds persists today. As even the godfather of lobbyists, Gerry Cassidy, observed, "it's mind-boggling that you can have a force like (hedge funds) in the market, have it be unregulated, and have members (of Congress) defending it being unregulated."[12] Mind-boggling, indeed; but perhaps Congress was simply responding to perverse incentives.

- America's business executives certainly understand the influence of money; in particular, as it relates to tax legislation. As Professor Lessig documents, "our tax code is riddled with the most absurd exceptions....proposed and secured by lobbyists."[13] An analysis of the impact of business lobbying concludes it is not "surprising that (corporations) spend.... money on lobbying since it has a quantifiable payoff in at least one important area, taxes. For firms spending an average of $779,945 on lobbying a year, an increase of 1% in lobbying expenditures produced a tax benefit of between

12 Robert G. Kaiser, *So Damn Much Money: The Triumph of Lobbying and the Corrosion of American Government* (New York, Knopf, 2009) p. 355

13 Ibid., p. 202

$4.8 million to $16 million… a 600%t to 2,000% return, not bad for government work!"[14]

This sampling of the corrupting influence of money on politics and policy is compelling evidence that America's ideal of market capitalism has devolved into crony capitalism—a distortion of market economics that benefits those who have the means and the will to use money to influence the behaviors (and the votes) of our representatives. Legality is not the issue. This is corruption of both democracy and free market capitalism, pure and simple. It transforms even the most well-meaning legislators from leaders to lackeys in thrall to money-supplying special interests. Equally important, the ability of these interests to influence policy in their favor allows a small percentage of Americans to enrich themselves as middle and lower incomes stagnate. As Cassidy admitted, "there has been a huge redistribution of income… it's just true, largely because they (poorer citizens) have less representation—you look at the movements out there, there is no anti-hunger movement…there is no committee on the Hill looking into poverty."[15] Perhaps Senator Bob Dole said it best, "poor people don't make campaign contributions."[16] Dole made this statement in 1982! Our corrupted system has been with us far too long, threatening our social stability and economic future. Until this changes, our system of values, democracy, and capitalism cannot operate either effectively or in a fair manner.

---

14 Ibid.

15 Kaiser, p. 355

16 Ibid.

Certainly this sampling of evidence makes it clear that our representatives and our businesses understand the influence of money. But what in our democratic governance allows this to happen? Some blame the controversial Supreme Court *Citizens United vs. FEC* decision. As Robert Post, Dean of the Yale Law School, states, "in effect the Supreme Court held that the loss of election integrity could never under any circumstances justify limitations on independent corporate campaign finance expenditures. It is beyond my comprehension how a responsible Court might regard electoral integrity as irrelevant to the protection of the First Amendment rights, and how it might regard history as irrelevant to the precious resource of electoral integrity. Electoral integrity is a foundational value for American democracy."[17] Regardless of whether you agree with the Court's decision or Post's opinion, it would be better to ask why it was that the Court, rather than our elected representatives, had to decide on a matter so fundamental to the integrity of the elective process.

If we believe that money has corrupted our system (and the previously provided examples would overwhelmingly suggest that this is the case), then it is the job of our representatives to protect the integrity of the process through legislation up to and including a constitutional amendment. This should not be a matter of legal interpretation. Rather, it is a fundamental question of values. In failing to address the issue of legal corruption, our representatives, and the minority of citizens who elect them, allow special interests to bias our system. The corruption goes beyond election contributions, requiring a comprehensive solution that minimizes the corrupting influence of money not just in elections but

17 Robert Post, *Citizens Divided* (Cambridge, Harvard University Press, 2014), p. 64

also in the performance of representatives once in office. Global citizen patriots need to understand the scope of representative corruption and the levers to be pulled to ensure that representatives are freed to work for "we the people."

Why American Representatives Are Corrupt

Here again, it is all about the money that has been allowed to decay our most fundamental and important democratic process: free elections. The various examples of corruption provided in the previous section are only outcomes of a badly flawed election system. This system controls who gets elected, how they perform while in office, and, in too many cases, how they use public service to create private rewards.

Who gets elected – It is expensive to run for public office (presidential, congressional, state legislative, or judicial elections). "Between 1974 and 2008 the average amount it took to run for reelection to the House went from $56,000 to more than $1.3 million. In 1974 the total spent by all candidates for Congress (both House and Senate) was $77 million. By 1982 that number was $343 million—a 450% increase in eight years. By 2010 it was $1.8 billion—a 525% increase again."[18] To get elected (or reelected), fundraising is the essential quid pro quo. The ever-increasing campaign costs of media spots and advertising, campaign staff, personal appearances, political consultants, and other expenses overwhelm attempts to survive on small average dollar amounts by mass donors. Rather, it is large individual, corporate, trade association, union, and other donors who foot the lion's share of the campaign bill.

18 Lessig, p. 91

There is something perversely democratic about a system in which the candidates who raise the most money enjoy advantage. For instance, it could be argued until recently that the most likely to be elected candidates often received contributions from the same sources (albeit in different amounts), allowing the funders access and influence regardless of the winner, but perhaps neutralizing the effect of their singular contributions on the actual election decision. However, after the 2010 Supreme Court ruling in *Citizens United vs. FEC*, it is impossible to accept this logic. In essence, the Citizens United decision gave corporations "the same right to make independent campaign expenditures that individuals had," giving them the right to spend an unlimited amount of money promoting or opposing a candidate. "Not surprisingly, we have seen an explosion in independent expenditures since that decision. Comparing 2010 to the last off-year election, spending is up more than 460%."[19] The current presidential election funding is dominated by the amounts of money pouring into super PACs. While the donors to these PACs often remain anonymous, it seems logical that the very largest contributors are betting on fewer horses, thereby creating a stronger dependence on the funder by the candidate. Given the amounts of money required, candidates simply cannot survive without the support (and influence) of these major donors. As Professor Lessig states, "there should be no doubt that an improper dependence now corrupts the institution of Congress." Rather than being dependent on, as Lessig describes, the "people alone," "the funders are not the people: the relevant funders of campaigns are less than .05% of America."[20] These funders largely determine who gets elected.

19 Ibid., pp. 238-239

20 Post, p. 102

How they perform in office – Once candidates reach office, the role of money continues in two important ways that impact how our representatives perform.

The first of these is the ability of lobbyists and other special interests to influence what gets debated and done in Congress. Referred to as "agenda corruption" by Professor Lessig,[21] the effect is that Congress works on issues important to their funders rather than those of the public interest. For example, Lessig refers to data contrasting the public's perception of the most important issues facing the country versus the priorities of lobbyists in their dealing with representatives. Notably, the three most important areas to the public (law, crime, and family policy; macroeconomics and taxation; and education) do not align with the lobbyists' focus on pushing the interests of their largest donors, most notably those in the fossil fuel, health care, financial, and transportation sectors.[22] The ability of these interests to deliver monetary support during the election and reelection processes provides that special interest with access to the representative. As former Representative Romano Mazzoli (Dem-KY) acknowledged, "people who contribute get the ear of the member ...access is power. Access is clout. That's how this thing works."[23] The effects of this access are demonstrated by legislation such as the Bankruptcy Abuse Prevention and Consumer Protection Act of 2005, which in essence prioritized the interests of credit card companies over the public by forcing debtors to repay their credit card debt before they paid child support or alimony. Lobbyist Gerry Cassidy referred to

21 Lessig, p. 142

22 Lessig, p. 143, Figure 11

23 Kaiser, p. 297

this as "the single worst piece of legislation from a public policy point of view that passed in recent years . . . and you have the banks, the credit card companies, driving the whole issue."[24] Money was the tool that allowed the financial services industry and their lobbyists to control the agenda, giving "$40 million to the campaigns of members to promote the new law over fifteen years. During the five years before the vote, the eighteen Senate Democrats who voted for the bankruptcy bill received, on average, $51,200 in campaign contributions from banks and credit card companies. Democratic senators who voted against the bill had received an average of $20,200."[25] Republicans and Democrats both received special interest money, but the highest bidders got the result.

The second form of corruption is one of distraction. Americans might reasonably expect their most senior representatives to spend the vast majority of their time performing their representative responsibilities. This is not the case. Professor Lessig cites numerous accounts that representatives spend between 30% to 70% of their time in office raising money, primarily for reelection.[26] The practical impact of this is that representatives have less time to meet with their broad constituency, attend committee meetings, or even attend congressional sessions. If the work of a congressman is "to debate, and listen, and argue, and then decide,"[27] many simply do not have the time to fully perform their essential duties. Rather, they are embroiled in seemingly permanent reelection campaigns, where attending to fundraising is a more valued function

---

24 Ibid., p. 301

25 Ibid.

26 Ibid., p. 138

27 Ibid., p. 140

within the parties than the advancement of policies and legislation that serve the broad public interest.

From public service to private rewards – Compared to the private sector, nobody gets rich on congressional pay (although most have to be rich and well connected to get there). Even after accounting for relatively expensive and extensive health, disability, and pension benefits, the 2015 base salary of $174,000 for rank-and-file members of the US House and Senate is paltry in comparison to executive pay in the private sector. Can we expect our congressional representatives to be the same quality as public sector executives if we pay them similar to mid-level managers? In a country where the average S&P CEO "pay package (in 2015) was $12.6 million,"[28] why would the best and brightest aspire to congressional service?

In theory, public service is a noble pursuit and attractive for that reason, even when one considers the corruption of our current elective and legislative processes. However, if we expect to attract the right representative talent, we need to pay them competitively or expect that they will seek additional benefits, compensation, or future job commitments to secure a family income and lifestyle at the level of other senior executives. Putting aside for the time being what a reasonable level of compensation might be for our most senior federal executives, we first need to recognize that the present corrupt system does in fact allow congressional representatives to get rich. While Hillary Clinton's estimated $12 million in speaking fees following her tenure as Secretary of

---

28 Mary Thompson, *This Is How Much More CEO's Make Than Workers*, CNBC.com (May 17, 2016)

State are impressive,[29] a more common path to post-Congress wealth is to become a lobbyist, a political consultant, or to work for an organization that desires access to politicians.

The access of retired congressmen to their former colleagues is a marketable commodity in a private market that equates access with power. "Between 1998 and 2004, more than 50% of (retiring) senators and 42% of House members made" the transition to lobbying. "In 2009 the financial sector alone had seventy former members of Congress lobbying on its behalf."[30] As former Congressman Jim Cooper related, "Capital Hill is a farm league for K Street. They expect to work for six to eight years making a salary just north of $160,000 a year. Then they want to graduate to a job making three to 10 times that amount as lobbyists. Their focus is therefore not so much on the people who sent them to Washington. Their focus is instead on those who will make them rich in Washington."[31] This career path to K Street has to influence even the most high-minded representatives.

Why are American representatives corrupt? The pervasive role of money in elections, the lobbyist-dominated legislative and reelection processes, and the opportunity to create post-congressional personal wealth distract representatives from their appointed tasks and corrupt their decision-making. The present system ensures that our representatives are lackeys to their funders while depriving America of the representative leadership it requires.

29 Maxwell Tani, "Here are all the six-figure speaking fees that Hillary Clinton received after leaving the State Department," *Business Insider* (May 20, 2015)

30 Lessig, p. 123

31 Ibid.

So, how do we get our representatives to work for all of us rather than their funders?

The Role of Representative Leadership

In his recent comprehensive and well-documented study of the history of modern states, *Political Order and Political Decay*, Francis Fukuyama decries the deterioration of American government. He cites imbalances between our executive, legislative, and judicial institutions that delay, deadlock, or under-resource effective policy making and execution. In particular, Fukuyama notes, "interest groups exercise influence way out of proportion to their place in society, distort both taxes and spending, and raise overall deficit levels through their ability to manipulate the budget in their favor."[32] These imbalances inhibit effective policy changes and result in "an overall system that allocates what should properly be administrative powers to courts and political parties. There is, in short, too much law and too much democracy relative to American state capacity."[33]

To Fukuyama, the inability of our legislative institutions to do their job is fundamental to their inability to represent the broad public interest. Instead, increasingly polarized special interests allow Congress to operate a vetocracy where one party or the other can stifle progress. He attributes this to two problems. First, political actors "have very deep interests in keeping things the way they are. Neither political party has

32 Francis Fukuyama, *Political Order and Political Decay: From the Industrial Revolution to the Globalization of Democracy* (New York, Farrar, Straus, and Giroux, 2014) p. 470

33 Ibid., p. 471

an incentive to cut itself off from access to interest group money, and the interest groups don't want a system where money no longer buys influence."[34] The second problem stems from the notion that "the typical American solution to perceived government dysfunction has been to try to expand democratic participation and transparency" despite the fact "that democratic publics are not in fact able by background or temperament to make large numbers of complex policy choices: what has filled the void are well-organized groups of activists who are unrepresentative of the public as a whole."[35] Populism is good when it causes people to vote, but policy making through referendums and other populist vehicles have proven themselves inadequate. Fukuyama highlights the essential role of a well-functioning bureaucracy and strong institutions in creating effective government. It is the leadership of effective representatives that needs to ensure that the government has the structures and the talent to manage our overall system. It is not about more or less government; it is about finding the right amount of government to serve the needs of the country.

Perhaps it is time to use the capitalistic methods and incentives of American business to address our political dysfunction. Central to any organizational change is the ability to understand the changes in the required skills and abilities, performance goals, and rewards and incentives that will ensure that representatives do what is needed. Just as in business, building a high-quality organization requires not simply the elimination of patronage and corruption. It also requires the creation of organizational capacity, starting with (in this case) representatives

---

34 Ibid., p. 504

35 Ibid.

who have the technical and emotional skills, support structures, and proper incentives to do the job. So, what should our representatives' role description look like?

Congressional Sample Position Description

What if we were to change the roles, accountabilities, and incentives of our representatives to ensure that they worked for us? In the private sector, organizational change is possible only after leadership has redefined the mission, vision, and values needed to drive future success. Supporting this mission with clear accountabilities, defining the needed technical and behavioral competencies needed, and reinforcing these with rewards that drive the needed actions are basic to any change program. If we expect our representatives to lead, we need to change their lackey-like roles and ensure that we are rewarding the leadership needed to create twenty-first-century America. Consider the impact of the following proposed congressional role description.

Organizational mission of congressional representatives – Balance the needs of their constituents and the broader needs of society with the overall goal of continuously improving America's system of values, democracy, and capitalism. Work in collaboration with other congressional members to organize and ensure the long-term growth of the country's five capital resources (physical infrastructure, financial assets, natural resources, human protection and development, and social stability, trust, and cooperation). Initiate, debate, and decide on policies to concentrate and redistribute the five capitals in ways that optimize opportunity for the maximum amount of citizens over the longest run.

Provide and continuously improve government organizational capability, structures, and procedures needed to engage and inform citizens, serve their immediate needs, and provide for their long-term security and advancement. Assist the executive function in promoting long-term global stability through the judicious use of American capital assets to lead mutual economic development and stability, enhanced security, and improved responses to crises and threats. Create a vision for America's future that builds on the values of our founders and continuously adapts our democracy and capitalism to the needs of all.

The representative role – Each elected representative of Congress shall serve a single (staggered) eight-year term with no reelection. The position will report to a panel of constituents and bipartisan peers who will annually evaluate the performance of the representative and the overall legislative bodies on the basis of pre-agreed, annually developed, short-term, and long-term measures of performance, adherence to organizational missions and values, and success in advancing America's domestic and global leadership effectiveness. Productive two-way communication and collaboration with the president and with leaders of the country's support bureaucracy (for example, National Institutes of Health and Center for Disease Control, Department of Commerce, Federal Trade Commission, Environmental Protection Agency, Food and Drug Administration, Securities and Exchange Commission, Internal Revenue Service, Social Security Administration, Veteran's Administration, Federal Communications Commission, Congressional Budget Office, etc.) are essential to ensure that basic public services are adequate, affordable, high-quality, and accessible to all who require them. Provide leadership and direction to staff members and ensure the continued development and management of a professional and efficient organization focused on serving constituent customers. Establish effective decision-making relationships and processes necessary to meeting congressional goals and objectives. Earn the trust of all citizens through the ability to clearly, and in a balanced manner, communicate the rationale for policy actions and their positive and negative implications. Regular interaction with diverse national and local media is important. In partnership with local constituents, help build a diverse and inclusive citizen representative group that is highly engaged and can serve as a vehicle for two-way communication between the representative and constituents. Regularly distribute information and position information to constituents and provide social media–based response vehicles to facilitate ongoing debate and discussion.

Key performance areas – Each representative shall be responsible for collaborating on a national business plan to set specific annual performance goals that balance the needs of local constituents and citizens countrywide. Performance areas should include each of the five capital areas with both long-term and immediate goals and measures of progress. Minimally, for example:

- Enhance **built capital** to improve twenty-first-century living and business conditions: Collaborate with other representatives, the president, state and local governments, and national support agencies to identify and recommend priorities for infrastructure and industrial investments with a clear statement of how these investments are intended to enhance the economy and the lives of citizens. For each investment, a clear cost and benefit analysis should be developed and shared with annual progress reports that report the current and desired state of essential infrastructure assets including, but not limited to, transportation, energy and power, water, waste disposal, air quality, communication, information and technology, etc. Invest in faster, cleaner, cheaper, and easier.

- Provide trustworthy and fiscally responsible **financial capital**: Ensure that the private financial sector is both adequately capitalized and precluded from assuming risks that would necessitate the use of public assets in the event of default. At the same time, ensure that all public retirement, health, and other obligations are actuarially projected with corresponding funding and investment plans that promote fair cost allocations across generations of citizens and balance the use of tax increases and benefit adjustments to provide adequate funding. Provide an annual assessment of private and public financing with specific goals for regulatory changes, tax and benefit level changes, the costs and benefits of changes, status of federal and state debt management, progress toward established goals, etc. Provide a stable, efficient, and non-predatory financial system that citizens can rely on to protect and grow their assets while allowing them to invest in better lives. In general, invest and reduce debt during good economic cycles, and invest and increase debt (to specified limits) in bad economic times—the best financial plans involve consistent investment.

- Leverage our **natural capital** for both citizens and businesses: Develop a comprehensive national plan to sustain and share our natural capital assets, in particular, clean water, air, and soil. Invest in efficient and non-polluting energy sources while altering the cost structures of fossil fuels to recognize the eventual costs of polluting externalities in the pricing of those fuels.

Create economic incentives and policies (business and home carbon taxes, cap and trade, for example) that will ensure adequate supplies of fair market–priced, fossil fuel–generated power until more sustainable, and less polluting, alternatives become available. Gradually raise the federal gasoline tax and eliminate subsidies to the fossil fuel industries that distort the true cost of these energy sources, using the increased funds to remediate pollution and enhance environment and citizen friendly programs and jobs (for example, national parks, environmental education, research and development for environmental technologies, etc.) and assist with the cost of infrastructure maintenance. Allocate public funds to environmental infrastructure cleanup programs that identify, prioritize, and remediate air, water, and soil environmental hot spots and threats. Ensure that all built capital uses the most advanced and efficient energy conservation methods and that citizens are aware of these opportunities. Preserve and manage plant, animal, and fish supplies to ensure adequate and sustainable resources, collaborating with other countries as needed to coordinate supply and demand. Provide citizens with an annual report stating progress toward natural capital enhancement goals, including a clear statement of the responsibilities and accountabilities of individual citizens.

- Develop our **human capital** to ensure that all citizens have the tools to succeed: Human capital development requires that all citizens have the opportunity to continuously enhance their individual technical and emotional skills, knowledge, and physical abilities. At the same time, citizens need to take responsibility for developing their abilities to communicate, listen, and think critically about values and policies. Each citizen must have opportunity coupled with accountability. It is the representative's role to ensure that a long-term plan is in place to ensure that America's human capital is both in adequate supply and developed to the highest levels possible. This may require radical changes to current ways of doing things. These changes should be carefully researched, debated, decided upon, and monitored. Representatives are responsible to review and reform the entire citizen creation process and enact changes that will, over time, create an engaged and informed citizenry.

For example, education systems have to serve our values, our democracy, and our economy. It is the role of the primary and secondary education systems (public and private) to ensure that basic skills and abilities are in place (recognizing special needs). Should these be a requirement before the rights of citizenship are granted? Should the basis for citizenship be changed from a birthright to requirements that, at a minimum, ensure citizen understanding of the responsibilities of citizenship, competency to execute those responsibilities, and participation in at least congressional and presidential elections? Should persistent failure to vote and perform certain other essential responsibilities (for example, military service, tax payments, jury duty, etc.) be the basis for disqualification of citizen status after reasonable notice and probationary periods? Should citizenship be earned, not given solely on the basis of birth location? These are fundamental questions that speak to how we view and value the roles of citizens. Beyond the basics of rights and responsibilities, citizens should have access to primary and secondary education systems that aspire to the highest global standards in all cases.

It is our representative's responsibility to treat education as an investment in our future rather than a cost to be minimized. At present, the funding of our school systems varies radically between school districts. In many cases, the reliance on property-valuation-related taxes has the effect of creating well-funded schools in affluent neighborhoods and funds-starved schools in the poorest neighborhoods. This creates a haves and have-nots education funding variance that reinforces racial, economic, and social inequalities. Policy makers are to develop plans to continuously increase and more evenly distribute the funds available to all public primary and secondary schools, increase the numbers and quality of teachers and administrators, take steps to promote more diverse (racial, social, and economic) student bodies, extend education programs to ensure that all schoolchildren are provided with adequate health promotion and nutrition programs regardless of their family situations, and increase the number of public/private partnerships (for example, internships, summer work, work/study programs, etc.) to improve the matching between curricula and the skills required to fill the full range of jobs once they complete secondary school. Make the education system a safety net to ensure the development of America's human capital as both citizens and contributors to their own, and society's, growth. Arguably, the development of this capital is the single most important component of our representatives' key responsibilities.

Finally, representatives need to develop a comprehensive immigration plan that better matches America's economic growth expectations with the necessary numbers of people of working age. At present, US birth rates and age demographics suggest a future shortfall of working-age people. Representatives are responsible for the development of comprehensive immigration reform that meets the needs of our economy and attracts and develops the most talented immigrants possible while ensuring national security.

- Promote a restructuring of our **social capital** systems to break down social barriers: It is time for representatives to prioritize social needs over those of special interests. When representatives prioritize the interests of credit card companies over those of spousal alimony and child support, something is clearly amiss. Representatives need to eliminate biased and regressive laws and policies in favor of a comprehensive social capital development program. The objectives of these changes should be to rebuild and remake our civil society (and the institutions that support society) in ways that, for example, promote family development, racial and economic integration and cooperation, community development, and improved trust and respect between religious groups, social movements, and advocacy groups. New policies should recognize that increasing numbers of single-parent households, fewer stay-at-home parents, increasing numbers of the aged relying on fewer working-age people for support, a dearth of middle-class jobs, and growing income inequality have outstripped the capabilities of America's current hodgepodge of social protections, volunteerism, religious affiliation, and charity. This suggests new roles for government, the private and the nonprofit sectors—roles that our representatives are responsible to define and orchestrate while earning the trust of constituents. As Fukuyama states, "putting loyalty to the state ahead of loyalty to family, region, or tribe requires a broad radius of trust and social capital. It is impossible to create social movements if people cannot be motivated to join civil society organizations, and they will not be inspired unless there is some ideal of civic responsibility to a larger community present among their fellow citizens."[36]

It is up to our government representatives to earn this trust by first divorcing themselves from the influence of special interests and then leading public debate concerning the roles of government and non-governmental organizations in building a new national-scope civil society based on trust in public and private institutions. It is then up to citizens to trust those representatives to balance the interests of all citizens in fair, transparent, and accountable ways. Fukuyama sees this debate and restructuring of civil society as an opportunity to effect more meaningful change to our social capital structures, noting that our response can be "more decisive because the decision to act is based on broader buy-in." It is a key representative accountability to "provide the substance of what people want from government: personal security, shared economic growth, and quality basic public services like education, health, and infrastructure that are needed to achieve individual opportunity."[37] Fragmented, under-resourced, and ideologically polarized institutions will

---

36 Ibid., p. 207

37 Ibid., pp. 546-547

not deliver this opportunity. Finally, our social capital will become increasingly fragmented if our representatives and their districts fail to represent all citizens. At present, gerrymandered voting districts distort electoral results and empower increasingly polarized groups. Most of all, gerrymandering results in underrepresentation of the poor and encourages their further disengagement from a political process in which they have less and less voice. As Robert Post states, "it is staggering to me that in the last general election only 47% of American voters cast their ballots for Republican representation in the House of Representatives, yet due in part to partisan gerrymandering the House ended up with a membership that was 54% Republican."[38] The implications for electoral integrity aside, this is no way to build the trust of the electorate. The development of social capital also depends on having political capital that is available to all on the same terms.

Representative qualifications – Executing the key responsibilities described in the previous section will require a range of capabilities. The representative role is a senior executive position that demands the highest level of technical skills and emotional competencies. A minimum of 10 years of government, business, and/or nonprofit experience, preferably in increasing leadership roles, is required. The following qualifications are applicable:

- Minimum of a university degree, ideally an advanced degree, or equivalent professional experience

[38] Ibid., p. 207

- At least 5–10 years of overall professional experience (business, nonprofit, government)

- Prior capital asset management (that is, the five capital areas) experience ideal; multiple asset management experience preferable

- Deep expertise in one or more capital asset areas preferable

- Significant experience in people/human capital development, communication and outreach, and fiscal management a must

- Technical competencies, including understanding of financial and political systems, strong analytic and problem-solving capabilities, business planning and organizational design and development experience, and track record as an effective leader

- Emotional competencies, including strategic thinking, coalition-building, ability to work effectively with diverse and potentially conflicting interests, negotiation and persuasion abilities that achieve consensus and compromise

- Outstanding presentation and two-way communication skills; a relationship builder

- Strong commitment to the development of staff and the overall organization; track record of recruiting and developing talent

- Global perspective, including the ability to understand and operate effectively in multicultural and multi-country environments

- Personally modeling the essential values of an effective representative leader: highest ethics, integrity, team player, positive and can-do spirit, the ability to discern and balance the needs of all, and the willingness to take positions and do the right thing

- Must have a track record as an active citizen

America is a talent-rich country. How can we ensure that the right amount of executive talent chooses to perform the difficult responsibilities of representative leadership?

Getting Representatives to Work for "We the People"

If we expect representatives to be attracted to this role, all of their compensation and rewards must come from the people. If we expect to attract the best talent, this compensation needs to reflect the market rate for that talent. If we expect representatives to be unbiased, all outside forms of compensation and perquisites need to be forbidden.

At the federal level, a suggested first step is to increase congressional rank-and-file salaries from $174,000 per year to a tax-free $1,000,000 per year (10% additional for party leaders of each house and the Speaker of the House). While this salary would pale in comparison to the multimillions paid to US CEOs and other business executives, it will certainly increase the pool of candidates who have the talent and the public service motivation to serve as representatives. At the same time, an executive pay level will reduce motivation to seek money elsewhere. In addition to salary, representatives would receive tax-free life, health, and disability benefits, a 5% tax-deferred annual retirement contribution, and a flat housing allowance of $50,000 per year. A reasonable, fixed-dollar allowance shall be established to cover direct travel and other expenses. All of these funds will be paid from federal monies. No forms of external compensation (for example, speaking fees, trips, meals, or gifts paid for by special interests, contributions made to others on behalf of the representative of his family, etc.) are permitted during the representative's time in office. Representative compensation and the housing allowance shall be indexed to appropriate cost of living indices. Finally, all representatives are precluded from entering into any form of post-congressional employment with lobbyists, political consultants, or as a lobbyist for any business interest. All representatives are required to sign a statement of ethical standards, responsibilities, and limitations making it clear that their allegiance is to the general public and that they agree to forego all forms of implicit and explicit outside compensation while in office.

The term for congressional representatives should be adjusted to a single eight-year term with no reelection of existing congressional members.

Assuming 435 House members and 100 members of the Senate, the approximate incremental cost to provide this pay increase would be $468,660,000. These funds will be paid from federal monies.

It is intended that state governments follow a similar model, adapted to the unique aspects of each state.

Freeing the Election Process from Corruption, Bias, and Ignorance

It is not enough to simply attract and reward the right people and have them do the right job. In addition, as Yale Law School Professor Robert Post states, "Electoral integrity is a foundational value for American democracy. And there are good reasons to worry that electoral integrity is today under threat."[39] How is electoral integrity under threat? Look no further than the duopolistic grip on the process by America's two major parties and the ways that money is permitted to influence their views and the success (or failure) of their candidates.

There is nothing inherently wrong with political parties. The ability to thoughtfully organize positions on issues of public interest and create, debate, and communicate platforms that articulate consolidated policies designed to support these positions are important and needed services to citizens. Having multiple parties with different platforms has the potential to provide citizens with choices that are better organized and articulated than otherwise might be the case. In addition, having candidates who commit to party platforms provides voters with some assurance that, once elected, the candidate will follow through on campaign promises.

In theory, parties best perform as public servants when they are ideological movements. In practice, as Post notes, "in the decades after the Civil War, however, American political parties began to lose their identity as ideological movements." Instead, "they came increasingly to seem organizations devoted chiefly to maintaining their hold on power."[40] This focus on retaining power distracts parties from their valued public service functions, and results in a situation, as described by Woodrow Wilson,[41] where "neither party has, as a party, anything definitive to say on these issues; neither party has any clean-cut principles, any distinctive tenets. Both have traditions. Both claim to have

39 Ibid., pp. 546-547

40 Ibid., p. 24

41 Ibid.

tendencies. Both have certainly war cries, organizations, interests, enlisted in their support. But those interests are in the main the interests of getting or keeping the patronage of government." As the political scientist J. Allen Smith stated, the party platform "ceases to be a serious declaration of political principles. It comes to be regarded as a means of winning elections rather than a statement of what the party is obligated to accomplish. Parties are thus essentially misrepresentative."[42] This misrepresentation undermines the integrity of the electoral process by focusing party leaders on securing the money and influence required to secure office. Arguably, this misrepresentation has only increased since the Citizen's United decision that has resulted in an explosion of opaque, well-funded super PACs whose only apparent purpose is to ensure that their funders receive priority at the government feeding trough.

Perhaps the 2016 presidential election process provides an opening for parties to reestablish credibility with voters. Consider the plight of the Republican Party. Saddled with a Trump candidacy that reflects the deep frustrations with establishment politics, is this a time for the party to rethink its traditional platforms to appeal to a broader demographic, and is it willing to work in concert with Democrats to reach compromise positions and get things done? What do the Republicans have to risk by presenting a bold plan for the future that appeals to a broader base? If Trump is to be crushed in a general election, wouldn't he and his party be better off to construct a platform that presents a more attractive future vision that is based on traditional conservative values but recognizes the need to be more inclusive and supportive of others? Can Trump's populist, anti-establishment appeal be channeled

---

42 Ibid., p. 27

by the party into specific platform commitments that address citizens' concerns about the role of money in elections and policy making? How refreshing would it be for the party platform to support public election financing and elimination of third-party money as suggested earlier in this chapter? Trump may be one of the least qualified presidential candidates in history. If he and his party are to appeal to a broad electorate, they could do worse than starting with a platform that promotes public election financing and reduction or elimination of the influence of special interests on policy development. This would not be easy, but it is likely to be popular, not only with dedicated Trump supporters but, more importantly, with a broader base of voters.

How could this be done? Consider Canada's restrictions on all campaign contributions and expenditures. In defending these restrictions, the Canadian Supreme Court "affirmed that individuals should have an equal opportunity to participate in the electoral process and that wealth is the main obstacle to equal participation." Further, the Canadian Court declared that campaign finance restrictions "promote an electoral process that requires the wealthy to be prevented from controlling the electoral process to the detriment of others with less economic power."[43] Evidently, the Canadian Supreme Court sees the influence of private money as a threat to their democracy, while the US Supreme Court interpretation of Constitutional First Amendment rights in Citizens United and other cases does not.[44] The point is that courts make decisions based on their interpretation of the legal facts and circumstances.

43 Ibid., p. 48

44 Post, pp. 48-49

While their interpretations might make sense from purely a legal sense, these interpretations may not always serve the interests of democracy.

It is the role of activist citizens and their representatives to ensure that our democratic processes—in this case, the election process—are as fair, participative, and unbiased as possible. If the US Supreme Court prioritized the right to First Amendment public discourse as part of the rationale for its Citizen's United decision, this does not prevent the Congress from clarifying, as the Canadian Supreme Court did, that "for voters to be able to hear all points of view, the information disseminated by third parties cannot be unlimited. In the absence of spending limits, it is possible for the affluent or a number of persons or groups pooling their resources and acting in concert to dominate the political discourse.... The unequal dissemination of points of view undermines the voter's ability to be adequately informed of all views."[45] The Canadians seem to be able to recognize and deal with the biasing effect of minority well-funded interests. Our representatives should be doing the same through legislative intervention, up to and including a constitutional amendment. The logic of this seems overpowering during an election process where well-funded interests are making unprecedented contributions to their favored candidates. No doubt they expect a return on their campaign contribution investment. And they probably will receive that return unless our representatives change the rules. How powerful would it be for the Republican Party platform to include a Canadian-style reform of the rules governing money in politics? Even if it ends up requiring a constitutional amendment.

45 Ibid., p. 79

Overturning the impact of Citizen's United is necessary but insufficient to promoting more democratic election processes. Imposing dollar limits on campaign contributions, providing public finances for elections, precluding contributions from corporations, unions, and other groups, changing voting districts to avoid partisan gerrymandering, and requiring free media time for candidates and election-related education are all tactics to be considered in what needs to be a comprehensive strategy of election reform. Essential to the creation of that comprehensive strategy is the input and direction of informed citizens. This input must go beyond the mere selection of representatives (although most do not currently participate in even that basic requirement of citizenship), requiring that all citizens participate in the elective process in as informed and active manner as possible.

These reforms represent incredible current opportunities for either or both parties. How many additional voters would be attracted to a party platform that commits to getting the money out of politics and that creates a less biased representative process that our founders would be proud of? Can parties ignore these potential voters?

What Gets Rewarded Gets Done

Redefining the roles, responsibilities, and accountabilities of representatives and appropriately rewarding them is the first step in allowing America to step away from partisan politics and the undemocratic influence of minority interests. Until we have the right talent doing the right job on citizens' behalf, we are unlikely to receive the leadership required to allow America to lead and prosper. This will not happen until we create a comprehensive and transparent system of rewards and accountabilities that reduces outside, biasing influences and focuses representatives on the maximum good for the most people over the longest time frame. What gets rewarded gets done. We need leaders, not lackeys, to do the job.

And Now for Citizens...

Perhaps the parties and candidates will yet play a productive role in reform as part of the 2016 presidential election, or in subsequent election processes. Global citizen patriots should not rely on this in the short term. How do citizens and representatives arm themselves with the wisdom to enact the right changes and adapt over time? There are actions citizens and representatives can take during the 2016 election process, and there are reforms that can support broader changes to our system. These are the subjects of the next chapter.

CHAPTER 6:
BRIDGING THE GAP: FIRST STEPS

The 2016 election opportunity—short-term citizen actions.

The Need for Short-Term Thinking

Restructuring our system of values, democracy, and capitalism is a long-term, ongoing project. Barring divine intervention, it is unlikely that citizens or representatives are simply going to wake up one morning and be inspired or feel empowered to change the system. Are there first steps that we can take; steps that will initiate confidence that we can create a future that provides the greatest benefit for the greatest number over the longest term? Can citizen and representative leaders create change momentum and initial successes that earn increasing confidence and support? Can present levels of cynicism and hopelessness be overcome? Most important, can a cadre of global citizen patriots provide the leadership essential to the first steps of change, thereby earning the credibility and the right to proceed with broader, system-wide changes? What specific first steps can be taken despite the present state of electoral and legislative dysfunction?

This chapter suggests actions that are within the grasp of citizens and their representatives right now. These actions can redefine the ways we think about values-based issues, improve the performance of our democracy, and better align our capitalistic economy with our values and democracy. At best, these actions are only the beginning of broader system-wide changes. Individual citizens, their representatives, their employers, the media, social activist groups, academia, and political parties all enjoy the independence to choose their positions and their actions. Are there leaders among these various cadres who can overcome the biases of money, influence, and power to act in the collective interest? What would their proposals and actions look like? What areas should these leaders focus on for maximum impact and proof of concept? In summary, how can global citizen patriots force initial changes to our constitutional, democratic, and capitalistic system that become the foundation for longer-term changes that will sustain and develop the vision of our founders?

From Populist Minorities to Patriotic Voters

The 2016 presidential election process underscores how frustrated Americans are with representative (congressional approval rates are at an all-time low) failure to develop and implement changes that will ensure that our nation's five capitals (resource, financial, built, human, and social) are developed and shared. Citizens are angered that special interests seem to control all important policy decisions. And they are increasingly convinced that money has hijacked the electoral process. This frustration and anger are both an opportunity and a risk.

To understand the risks, look no further than the campaigns of Donald Trump and Bernie Sanders. Both created viable candidacies despite positions that are nonsensical and a poor interpretation of traditional American values (in Trump's case) or, in Sanders's case, socially desirable to many but fiscally unrealistic. They were able to accomplish this through the support of partisans who are attracted, at least in part, to their supposed willingness to forego money from special interests. This freedom from the influences of traditional well-funded interests allows them to break from typical party rhetoric and methods to promote policies that play to the fears and concerns of their supporters. While neither Trump's nor Sanders's partisans represent a majority within even their own parties, this break from party control represents a real sea change from the past where the ability of the candidate to generate the vast majority of their campaign contributions from large donors and garner party support largely determined their electoral viability. Regardless of what you think of Trump and Sanders and their platforms, it is clear that both candidates have tapped into critical aspects of what makes Americans mad as hell: the inability of representatives to overcome the influence of money and the inability of candidates to speak openly about our problems. The passion and dedication of Trump's and Sanders's partisans is refreshing. But it is also dangerous.

One risk is the fact that neither candidate espouses positions that are likely to reflect the interests and preferences of a majority of Americans. This is particularly true in Trump's case, where his support comes from a fraction of the electorate who ignores his personal shortcomings, biases, and inconsistent policy ramblings, perhaps with the hope that his business orientation will allow him to make deals. The perception that Trump, not beholden to special interests, will be able to get things done after receiving the public's mandate in the presidential election, is no doubt empowering to those who believe, for example, that they have been disadvantaged as a result of freer trade, loosened immigration, the social advancement of non-white races, women, and those of differing lifestyle or religious preferences, and the failure of our allies to fairly share the cost of providing security. The ability to appeal to a distinct segment of the electorate during the primary process has created the possibility of a Trump presidency. Should a very motivated group of frustrated partisan voters determine this? Regardless of what the Republican establishment might do to moderate Trump's behavior and policy initiatives, the current presidential election process is what happens when citizen frustration finds expression through a candidate who preaches to a choir of partisans that he or she is not part of a political system that fails Americans. More important, the ability of a well-motivated minority constituency to determine a presidential nomination, and perhaps the presidency itself, is profoundly troubling. But it can only occur if large numbers of voters fail to participate in the presidential election.

Hard Choices and Truth Serum

The failure of voters to adequately participate in the primary processes, and even in the presidential election, is a problem that can only be addressed if citizens do their fundamental job of voting and making their opinions and frustrations publicly evident. In addition, candidates should turn the page on traditional party dogmas and acknowledge that the positive worldwide impact of globalization, while lifting many developing countries out of poverty, has not been uniformly applied to Americans. As *NY Times* columnist Roger Cohen hypothesized, "another two decades of neo-liberal, reward-the-rich, trust-globalization-to-deliver politics will lead to social breakdown, the triumph of demagogues, and perhaps mayhem. A rising tide may raise all yachts. It does not raise all boats."[1] Americans increasingly understand the fallacy of relying on out-of-date beliefs and policies that fail to produce reasonable levels of fairness, opportunity, and social stability. However, attempts to return to the past will not "make America great again." An electoral victory of one partisan group over another can only result in continued policy gridlock or, even worse, repression of the majority.

It is time for citizens and representative leaders to recognize both the benefits and the increased instability and inequality caused by globalization. Speaking the truth about the hard choices fomented by globalization is the first act of patriotism. As noted by Cohen, "Isaiah Berlin, who witnessed the ravages of Fascism and the destruction of Europe, wrote that, equality may demand the restraint of the liberty of those who wish to dominate; liberty—without some modicum of which there is no choice and therefore no possibility of remaining human as

---

1 Roger Cohen, *The New York Times* (April 4, 2016)

we understand the word—may have to be curtailed to make ready for social welfare, to feed the hungry, to clothe the naked, to shelter the homeless, to leave room for the liberty of others, to allow justice or fairness to be exercised." Steven Weisman, in his book *The Great Tradeoff: Confronting Moral Conflicts in the Era of Globalization*, defends the moral case for continued economic globalization that has lifted billions out of poverty while noting "the conflicts between ensuring economic justice for one's own community and ensuring it for others in the world at large, especially the world's poorest citizens."[2] This is a tough sell if you are part of an American middle class where the effects of globalization have often been loss of jobs to overseas workers and wage stagnation. Economic justice is unevenly applied by globalization. If we expect the losers from globalization, in this example the American middle class, to support continued globalization (with its promise to lift additional, albeit remote, billions out of poverty), it is up to our system of values, democracy, and capitalism to support citizens faced with the difficult economic realities of continued globalization.

The forces of globalization are a tide that will not be denied. Politicians who say that they can insulate America from globalization's implications are poor servants of America's, and the world's, long-term interests. Global citizen patriots need to understand the negatives associated with globalization and support candidates who are both forthright about these problems and supportive of policies that mitigate, at the country level, the economic damage caused by globalization. As Weisman states, "what many forget is that several other principles would fall under the heading of economic justice, an essential ingredient if the public is to

2 Steven R. Weisman, *The Great Tradeoff: Confronting Moral Conflicts in the Era of Globalization* (Washington, DC, Petersen Institute for International Economics, 2016) p. 3

support such efforts. These principles include greater spending on basic health and education for poor or troubled countries, and tax reform, specifically broadening taxes to combat crony capitalism and corruption and to ensure that the wealthy pay their fair share." Candidates who play to partisan groups opposing globalization or promise lots of additional social benefits without the taxes to pay for these changes are deceiving the electorate. If we support the greatest possible gains for the greatest number over the longest term, we need to recognize that there will be winners who need to share their winnings and losers who will need assistance. Politicians who ignore compromise and tough trade-offs are partisans. Representatives who articulate the challenges while advocating changes that are fair to the demos as a whole are global citizen patriots. And the balance they advocate is the foundation of liberty and justice for all.

As the presidential primaries ended and the general election process unfolds, most American voters will have lost the opportunity to express their opinion where it most matters—at the polls or in caucuses. This is a huge risk to our democracy in that it makes it possible for minority populists to select candidates who are not representative. In theory, this problem is minimized if a large majority of the electorate turns out to vote in the presidential election. But what happens if both presidential finalists are partisan, rather than majority, candidates? Perhaps we owe a debt of gratitude to candidates like Trump, who, by being so divisive, has motivated many apolitical citizens to pay attention to and participate in the election processes. Voter awareness and participation is the essence of democracy, and 100% voter participation is the enemy of subversive special interests and the foundation of representative democracy.

It is too late to change the fractured state-by-state processes of primaries and caucuses for this election cycle. But it is not too late for all citizens to vote in the presidential election. Our democracy is at significant risk. Global citizen patriots are the last line of defense. Vote or accept the consequences.

Do Parties Work for Parties or Citizens?

The 2016 election has highlighted a second risk to our democracy: our two political parties conduct nominating processes in which the parties have more say about the winner than do the voters. The insurgent Trump candidacy has done us a favor in calling this risk to attention. If you are a Trump supporter, the mobilization of the Republican Party in support of any alternative other than Trump has to be disturbing in its seeming unfairness. Indeed, a candidacy that garners the majority of the nominating delegates and the biggest single group of the primary popular vote only to have had the possibility of defeat at a convention where party rules and bylaws could have resulted in the selection of a candidate with fewer delegates or, worse, a candidate who had not participated at all in the primary vetting process—the fact that this is at all possible begs the question of whether this process is wholly democratic. Votes are supposed to count ("by the people").

The *New York Times*, no supporter of Trump, in an April 4, 2016, editorial observed, "elections of all sorts rest not on rules and bylaws but on legitimacy."[3] However, both parties have crafted nominating rules that, while ostensibly intended to prevent the nomination of non-viable

---

3 Charles Blow, "The (Un)Democratic Party," *The New York Times* (April 4, 2016)

or unrepresentative candidates, probably better serve the party's ability to select the eventual nominee. In the Republican Party's case, it seems that they relied on the rules governing the selection and voting instructions of convention delegates to defeat a potential Trump nomination. When this failed to achieve the party's objective, there was talk of changing the rules in ways that would facilitate Trump's defeat. While to many, this may seem a justifiable solution in light of Trump's shortcomings, citizens need to question an election process that results, despite great expense of time and money, in nominees who are so onerous to their own party that the party feels the need, and has the ability, to fix the outcome.

The Democratic Party nomination process is equally rule-bound and potentially undemocratic. In the aforementioned op-ed of April 4, 2016, Charles Blow describes two ways in which the Democratic presidential selection process has the potential to subvert democracy. In contrast to the Republican process, in which convention delegates were (at least initially) chosen as a result of voter input during the primaries, 712 Democratic convention delegates were appointed solely by the party. These delegates were not pledged, being able to vote for any candidate regardless of the popular voting during the primaries. As Blow states, "super delegates, whose votes are not bound by the millions of individual voters, make up nearly a third of all delegates. That, on its face, is outrageous. The system is unjust, in part because the super delegates are not prohibited from declaring their loyalty before voting has ended. At the very least, they should be barred from committing before voting is completed in their own states. Without this prohibition, the establishment puts its thumb on the scale and signals its approval and disapproval ahead of Democratic voters. How can this be defended?"

In practical terms, 359 superdelegates committed to Hillary Clinton nearly three months before a single vote was cast (versus eight for Bernie Sanders). The party had spoken loudly and clearly about who their candidate should be. Perhaps Clinton will be an excellent president. However, the influence of superdelegates in the nomination process undermines her credibility and feeds mistrust. Our election processes should do the opposite.

Blow, in the same op-ed, also questions the efficacy of caucuses. While his article focuses on the Democratic caucuses, his logic applies to the caucuses of both parties. Noting restrictive voting hours, the lack of privacy and anonymity of the voting booth, and state-by-state inconsistencies in rules, delegate allotment, and proxy balloting, Blow concludes that "for a Democratic Party that prides itself on the grand idea of inclusion and fairness, the nominating process is anything but."

It is unlikely that most citizens could describe the complex and different sets of rules governing the Republican and Democratic nominating processes. Perhaps many citizens fail to focus on this as they have confidence that voters will have the final say in the presidential election (the Electoral College notwithstanding). But what happens when neither party's candidate is representative of even a single party's majority? Are we convinced that parties truly work in the interest of the demos? Or should we be concerned that they exist more to win elections and promote the interests of those who fund their campaigns?

If the Democratic and Republican parties are supposed to be the representatives of citizen interests in the creation of platforms and policies and in the selection of candidates, what insulates them from the well-funded special interest corruption evident in Congress? At this point, it appears that one defense against party manipulation is for voters to rebel against traditional, party-line nominees. The current election process has no doubt been a wake-up call for party leaders as they attempt to deal with insurgent candidates such as Trump and Sanders. It can only be hoped that the same wake-up call will occur for voters in the general election. Only by turning out in unprecedented numbers can Americans have any assurance that the outcome will be at least somewhat representative of their preference.

Parties can also reform themselves. How refreshing would it be for either party's platform to commit to a review and reform of their nomination processes in time for the next presidential election? More uniform state-by-state primary processes, elimination of winner-take-all delegate selection, extension of voting rights to independents, the ability to vote by mail, the elimination of superdelegates, and transparent rules on all these processes would greatly enhance the credibility of the overall nomination process and demonstrate that the party is serious about democratic values.

Democracy is hard. Both the ends and the means are important. When the methods of democratic elective choice are so complex and party-controlled that the demos is suppressed, it is time to debate how we might change the rules. The parties have the power to do this; citizens should urge them to act. But until we change the rules, Americans need to vote.

Making the 2016 Election Work for Citizens

The risks to our democracy described in the previous section will be mitigated by large presidential voter turnouts. This part is up to "we the people." But what else can be done over the short-term course of the 2016 election to help ensure the best possible outcome while planting the seeds of eventual changes to the corrupted representative processes described in previous chapters? Are there actions that global citizen patriots can take now to influence the election in ways that help citizens make the best possible voting choices while sending a message to the political system and its leaders (Congress, party leaders, special interests, etc.) that they need to commit to, or at least accept, fundamental changes that will promote an improved democracy?

Here are seven ideas that citizens (and representatives!) can advocate or do: things leaders can support as a way of positioning themselves as the global citizen patriot leaders of change.

- **Let's compete on ideas rather than ideology** – It is easy to be consumed by the passions of the current election process. Citizens have strongly held and ingrained beliefs on both sides of policies on immigration, the role of government, the extent of social network protections, and so on. If anything, the candidates and their parties are more polarized than ever. There is an alarming amount of inflammatory rhetoric with little attempt at balanced debate and discussion as candidates feel the need to play to influential sectors of their constituencies rather than attempt to represent the general best interest. Candidates focus on issues that consolidate their core support, offer sharp contrasts (versus middle ground suggestions) to the opposition, and play to media attention. Attacking the opposition seems to always garner more attention than well-conceived, articulated, and collaborative policy suggestions. Paraphrasing Arthur C. Brooks, president of the conservative American Enterprise Institute, "the current polarization in America obstructs this kind of collaboration. First, the solution starts not with institutions, but with individuals. We look too much to political parties or Congress to make progress, but not nearly enough at our own behavior. Second, liberals should be liberals and conservatives should be conservatives. But our duty is to be respectful, fair, and friendly to all, even those with whom we have great differences."[4] Can we expect candidates to engage in fair play, respect, and the politics of compromise in the service of progress if we as individuals fail to do so? Brooks suggests, "the next few months are an opportunity for people who care about politics and policy. Each of us can be one part of the solution America needs to become a more pluralistic, tolerant country, in which differences are part of a competition of ideas, not a ghastly holy war of ideologies." Let's behave in ways that demonstrate the best elements of our founders' values. This starts with respect and caring for all reasonable expressions of how we might improve the American system. Being an effective global citizen patriot surely requires an objective, truth-seeking focus on ideas versus slavish adherence to ideology. A platform of both respect and ideas should be voters' starting point when evaluating candidates. Forget party allegiances. Which candidates offer the best ideas and deliver them in a respectful manner? When

---

4 Ibid.

citizens begin to insist on ideas rather than ideologies, and collaborative action versus partisan gridlock, sensible politicians will take their cues accordingly.

- **Every citizen votes** – The 2016 presidential election has exposed the influence of motivated minority interest groups and the control that Democratic and Republican party elites exercise on the process. In the latter case, these parties' ability to influence the eventual nominees through appointment of party elite superdelegates, the state-by-state ability of the party to influence convention delegates who are not bound to primary popular vote after the first ballot, winner-take-all primaries that give all delegates to one candidate rather than allocate delegates in relation to the popular vote, the inability of independents to vote in states like New York, and the ability to change the nominating convention rules at any point—all of these give the parties, rather than the people, disproportionate influence. In the short run, the only possible defense against this undemocratic party hegemony is if the vast majority of citizens turn out to vote in the presidential election. Only then can citizens enjoy reasonable hope that a measure of democracy will be retained. While it is still possible that the Electoral College system can result in a minority presidency, the backlash from this outcome (in terms of popular outrage and media exposure) could serve as the spark for discussion of changes that can reform the election process, reassert the primacy of the popular vote in the primary and presidential selection processes, and allow the formation of new parties who might better represent large citizen constituencies. Uniform state-by-state primary methods and rules, the ability to form third-party movements (essentially blocked today by a dizzying array of rules and laws passed by the parties to effectively exclude third-party movements), and a reevaluation of the efficacy of the Electoral College are all needed if we are to ensure that our democracy is not overcome by the power of parties more interested in winning further power and influence in the service of their most significant funders than in representing the needs of American citizens as a whole. Changes to our election processes should be taken only after great debate and consensus seeking. But the momentum and the impetus for those longer-term changes will not come until the majority exerts its ability to stand up in the presidential election process and ensures that the people's will, and not the preferences of party elites, controls the outcome. The first step in reforming the election processes is to make it clear to the parties that appealing to the voters takes priority over appealing to their donors. Vote, get your family members to vote, encourage your neighbors, coworkers, and friends to vote and let candidates know that you are not only "mad as hell" but that you expect them to do something about it. Take the first step in becoming a responsible global citizen patriot—vote.

- **Get the money out of the process prospectively** – The 2016 presidential election will be the most money-driven election in history. It is too late to get the money out. But global citizen patriots can take the first steps to ensure that this is the beginning of the end of the corrupting influence of money on our democracy. The solution is straightforward: public election financing supplemented by limited (for example, $1,000 maximum) contributions by individual voters. Organizations (for example, corporations, not-for-profit businesses, super PACs) would be precluded from any form of contributions to candidates. We could do worse than to emulate the rules that govern the current Canadian election process. Given the US Supreme Court decision on *Citizens United vs. FEC,* it is possible (and perhaps desirable) that this can only be accomplished via Constitutional Amendment. This is a long-term process that requires debate, clarity on the best ways forward, and voter consensus. However, the time to begin that debate is now. Global citizen patriots, enlightened leaders, and the media can make their preferences on public election financing, in whatever form, clear during this presidential election, demanding that candidates address the issue and state a position. Putting candidates on the spot during this election, making it clear that future congressional candidates will be subject to the same questions, is the first step in letting candidates know that future electability will be at least partially influenced by their espousal of a private/public election financing method that minimizes the influence of well-funded special interests. How refreshing would it be to have the eventual winner in the 2016 presidential election state, during his or her inaugural address, that they will no longer accept contributions from lobbyists, their clients, corporations, individuals, super PACs, or anyone else in excess of $1,000 as part of any reelection effort? At the same time, the newly elected president should call on all other candidates in the next election to do the same and invite a debate on increasing public funds for that next election. Bernie Sanders's campaign has suggested that it is possible to raise adequate funds from the general public to support a presidential candidacy. This type of inaugural statement could be a game changer. It would also be the act of a courageous global citizen patriot leader.

- **Identify fact-based and diverse sources of information** – It is impossible to avoid biased information. Mainstream media is often more concerned with attracting viewers and advertisers than objectivity. Partisan Internet sites play to special interests and groups that share their biases and opinions, preaching to a choir of loyalists who become more and more convinced of the sanctity of their beliefs. Facts to support just about any position are ubiquitous. But where is rational and balanced debate? Social media perpetuates bias. Users of Facebook, for example, tend to "friend" others who see eye-to-eye with them on social positions and politics. Certainly there are some fascinating debates on Facebook about candidates, politics, and social positions. However, if you are "unfriending" people who disagree with you, if you are posting articles supporting your positions and these articles are always from the same sources, or if you always support any position taken by a particular special interest group, you need to rethink your objectivity and ability to compromise in the public interest. Overdosing on Fox News, MSNBC, or NRA publications? Find the *NY Times* too liberal or the *Wall Street Journal* too conservative? Try the PBS News Hour, the BBC World News, *The Economist* magazine, or *Foreign Affairs* bi-monthly publications for a change. All sources of information have inherent bias of some sort. But the aforementioned suggested sources seem to at least attempt to put journalism first and viewer numbers and advertising revenue second. In this age of information, information bias is a formidable enemy of democracy. The ability of citizens to access a dizzying number of information sources is a First Amendment right. But it is the ability (indeed, the responsibility) of citizens to wisely choose their sources and derive balanced, objective positions that form global citizen patriots who can advocate and support the changes that can create the greatest good for the greatest number over the longest term. Certainly, this information management problem cannot be addressed overnight. But the first step in the cure is awareness of the problem and willingness to try additional information feeders that will expand viewpoints. Thoughtful consumers of media are better citizens. Critical thinking matters. Start today.

• **Clarify and leverage the things we agree on** – The ferocity of partisan politics can obscure the fact that Americans, regardless of their party allegiances and ideological differences, agree on much more than they disagree on. Our Constitution and Bill of Rights are foundational to how we operate our democracy. Our capitalistic system has been the envy of the world in its historical ability to distribute economic opportunity (albeit unevenly) while growing GDP per capita. Most of all, Americans understand and support the essential dimensions of our values. These include fairness supported by rule of law, altruism that supports basic social protections for all, military strength to ensure our security, an education system that offers opportunity to all, adequate environmental protections to ensure clean air and water and protection of biological entities, and a capitalistic economy that balances business profits and societal prosperity. Clarifying the things we agree on is an important anchor if we are to embark on change discussions.

- Change does not come easily to Americans. Entrenched interests, nostalgia for former times, political gridlock, and legitimate differences on the best ways forward all conspire to slow, and sometimes defeat, change. Yet, in a rapidly changing world, failure to adapt our system is neither an option nor a prescription for progress. Election candidates thrive on the message of change, but we lack the tools to identify change priorities, make choices, and manage ongoing change. As corporations know, effective change management requires resources and infrastructure. If we are to prioritize, debate, choose, and implement the changes needed to sustain and progress American values, democracy, and capitalism, we need forums that can diagnose our most pressing priorities and debate solutions. In *Republic, Lost*, Professor Lessig suggests that citizens call for a modern-day constitutional convention (this requires the approval of thirty-four states if it is to address constitutional issues) to surface and debate these issues.[5] A contemporary version of our original constitutional convention is a great idea. What do citizens risk by insisting on this? And, even if thirty-four state approvals cannot be obtained, what is to prevent universities, media sources, and global citizen patriots, for example, from sponsoring mini-conventions on issues relating to needed changes in the American system? Looking for additional stimulus and leadership for the concept of conventions? An excellent idea to include in our next president's inaugural speech—proposing funding for multiple issue-specific conventions that will engage the public in balanced dialogue concerning the most important issues facing our country. Or an excellent grant opportunity from

5 Lawrence Lessig, *Republic, Lost* (New York, Hachette Book Group, 2012) pp. 300-304

some of our most wealthy citizens and their foundations. Let balanced and informed public debate determine what is important, state what we agree on, and define compromise alternatives for the things we are unable to agree on. That's democracy.

- **Enlist the forces of capitalism** – Business has always played an important leadership role in the adaptation of America. At their capitalistic best, American businesses have created good jobs that supported the development of a strong middle class, have driven incredible advances in technology, medicine, finance, and many other areas that have created both long-term shareholder value and employee wage increases while demonstrating incredible ability to adapt, most recently from an industrial-dominated to a services-focused economy. American companies compete effectively with a combination of leading-edge management skills, access to capital and ability to create earnings, ability to globally organize, develop, and deploy human capital, and create and deliver products and services through ever-adapting global supply and delivery chains. They are, in the aggregate, the most recognized, popular, diverse (in terms of industry grouping), and valuable worldwide brands. Yet, all too often, American companies fail to create market reputations that live up to these brands. Consider the reputation damage suffered by financial institutions during and after the 2008 financial crisis, the public relations issues that technology companies have experienced as a result of moving domestic jobs to low-cost countries with substandard labor practices, and the infuriating (at least to the average tax payer) tax avoidance and evasion strategies practiced by many organizations, particularly when these tax-favored benefits have resulted from tax benefits or subsidies derived from the influence peddling of well-paid lobbyists. Also consider the declining engagement of American workers with their employers. While this is often attributed to the changing work habits and expectations of new generations of American workers, better documented culprits are the significant number of US jobs that have been, and will continue to be, lost to automation. According to a Citigroup/Oxford study, 47% of the US workforce is at risk of job loss through automation; job losses that will not be offset by new industries. Further, these new industries will require better education, both confining these jobs and resulting in a disproportionate share of high pay and high wage increase jobs accruing to a small pool of very highly educated workers in science, technology, engineering, and mathematics (STEM), management, and select industries. Perhaps, quite logically, American workers find it difficult to engage with jobs that offer little opportunity for advancement and high risk of elimination. The challenges of competing in today's global markets coupled with the expectations of job losses through automation and continued globalization of the workforce are a significant threat to both American businesses and to American workers, in terms of potential social instability caused by lack of employment opportunity and underemployment, reduced purchasing capacity of consumers, reduced business profits, and increased business uncertainty that adversely affect investment decisions. All of this occurs at a time when accumulated US national debt has reached dangerously high levels. In fact, "the Congressional Budget Office projects that if current tax and spending policies continue, the US debt-to-GDP ratio will rise to 128% of GDP in 2030 and more than 200% of GDP in 2050, a level economists say will produce inflation, lower growth, unemployment, and possible financial crises."[6] All of these projections should be sobering. If we can no longer rely on business to deliver the jobs and pay levels needed to create meaningful work and compensation, if businesses are constrained by ever-increasing competition and are concerned about the impact of social instability, and the government is less able to step in with financial assistance, is it time to rethink the public/private partnership between US government and American business? If American businesses and entrepreneurs are unlikely to create adequate, meaningful jobs in the future (or even if there is the risk of this), we need to begin debating alternative strategies that reset the ways in which business and the government work together to develop the nation's human capital.

- **Know what we can afford** – Citizens need to understand the high-level arithmetic of our federal and state budgets. Jeffrey Sachs provides an excellent summary of government revenues and outlays in *The Price of Civilization: Reawakening American Virtue And Prosperity.*[7]Sachs estimated 2015 government revenues and expenditures as a percent of GDP—18% and 24%, respectively. He started "with a baseline structural budget deficit of 6% of GDP" and concluded "that the United States will need substantially more revenues to close the budget deficit, especially recognizing the need to increase federal spending in certain critical areas."[8] This large structural deficit and the national debt (and large interest payment that result) require changes if we are to pay

---

6 Weisman, p. 112

7 Jeffrey D. Sachs, *The Price of Civilization* (New York, Random House, 2011) pp. 209-231

8 Ibid., pp. 220-221

for needed programs and invest in our future. With the Congress hopelessly deadlocked in partisan battles, it is in every citizen's interest to have an understanding of the sources and uses of our federal and state budgets. Only then can we have a sensible debate concerning the tough trade-offs between what we would like to provide and what we can afford. For example, what combination of personal income, payroll (Social Security, Medicare, unemployment, etc.), sales (gasoline, state and local, etc.), business and other taxes, and state and federal expenditures (e.g., the military, Medicaid, government employees, etc.) will allow the country to operate at sustainable financial levels of annual debt and gradually reduce current levels of national and state debts (and their related interest costs) to acceptable, affordable, and sustainable levels?

What public investments in infrastructure modernization, education, research and development, and human capital and jobs development does America need to make to support business? At the same time, how can businesses better support the economy through labor development and retraining programs, paying their fair share of taxes, improved collaboration on wage setting for low-wage earners and executives, and renouncing campaign contributions as an investment to secure favored tax, regulatory, or other treatments? American businesses enjoy competitive advantages created by public funding; access to highly educated talent from American universities, use of public transportation systems, access to the nation's abundant natural resources, the security provided by effective rule of law and the world's strongest military, and reasonably effective government bureaucracies that support rather than inhibit business creation and growth. There is a cost to all these benefits that businesses need to help pay for.

What is the optimal balance of cuts to existing government programs and increase in taxes that will produce the desired budget result over time? Who are the winners and losers in terms of who will pay more in taxes and/or lose entitlements versus those who will benefit from increased expenditures or reduced taxes? What is the value proposition to both the winners and the losers that will cause them to support the specified changes?

At present, special interests cloud any debate of the trade-offs that will require some individuals and businesses to pay more and some to pay less.

Let's consider the following four initial strategies to support national fiscal responsibility and provide businesses with cost relief in some areas.

1. Maintain the world's most effective military and reduce defense spending.

2. Provide universal health care to all citizens but manage care in ways that reduce the nation's private and public (Medicare and Medicaid) health costs as a percent of GDP.

3. Stabilize Social Security by increasing taxes and delaying benefits for wealthier Americans.

4. Simplify the tax code to reduce taxes for the poor while eliminating tax benefits that disproportionally benefit the rich (most notably the mortgage deduction) and certain industries.

We can reduce our national budget deficits, spend more to stimulate business, and reduce poverty and inequality. Other countries like Canada and northern European countries do this. Yes, they do pay higher taxes as a percentage of GDP. But they get a lot in return—and their national happiness levels are higher.

The Time for Action Is the Present—and the Future

The 2016 election process has been remarkable in demonstrating the extreme frustration of Americans with the dysfunction of our constitutional, democratic, and capitalistic system. Wise politicians will absorb the lessons learned from the populist Trump and Sanders movements; that is, Americans are "mad as hell" and new ideas matter. Let's hope that the remainder of the election process will see the emergence of representatives who are willing to swear off the money that clouds public interests, speak the truth about America's hard choices, and suggest a vision of the future that will, rather than make America great again, make it greater than it has ever been. Voters and enlightened representatives can make a difference in the short term.

However, renouncing dependence on special interests, reforming political party nomination processes, speaking the truth about our shortcomings, 100% voter turnout in the presidential election, and even an uplifting inaugural speech will not change the system. Nor will it overnight create global citizen patriots who can debate, represent, and support change. This is a longer-term process. That longer-term process is the subject of the following chapter.

CHAPTER 7:
REALITY TV FOR TWENTY-FIRST-CENTURY
GLOBAL CITIZEN PATRIOTS

Emerging from twilight—citizens are created, not born.

Forming a Better Long-Term System of
Constitution, Democracy, and Capitalism

Chapter 6 recited a number of short-term strategies to channel the populist fervor of the 2016 presidential election into productive platforms for change. A large voter turnout is the best way to ensure a consensus winner and reduce the risk that gerrymandered districts and states or the Electoral College will determine the result. In the face of huge voter turnout, wise candidates (and hopefully their parties, as well) should grasp the fact that election results will be tied to their ability to appeal to the broadest base of voters. Hence, their willingness to moderate positions, find common ground, and compromise in the interests of the overall demos while acting independently of special interests is the type of leadership most likely to garner a majority of voters.

Is the 2016 election the beginning of a period of change when both the Democratic and Republican parties need to alter their focus from winning elections and serving their financiers to actually working for the demos? How refreshing is it that Trump (at least initially) and Sanders distanced themselves to varying degrees from traditional party politics and large donors? Perhaps Trump's constantly shifting policies and personal behavior are unacceptable and certain of Trump's and Sanders's economic policies are economically bankrupt. However, the enthusiasm of their supporters suggests that "voters want elected officials who will work with each other for the common good, rather than craven careerists who chase campaign contributions and vote accordingly or zealots who prize ideological purity over results."[1] Will Hillary Clinton break from her perceived mold as a career politician beholden to special interests? Is she willing to be truly courageous—taking positions on the need for improved national fiscal responsibility, acknowledging that we need to make budget cuts in some areas while investing in others, or advocating for trade policies that alleviate global poverty but cost US jobs? Trump, Sanders (who has influenced the Democratic platform regardless of the nomination outcome), and Clinton have an opportunity to break from business-as-usual politics and policies. Are they willing to advocate public financing of elections and redefined representative roles and compensation as described previously in this book? Will the Libertarian third-party candidate exert influence on the election by presenting a more appealing platform that is less the work of

1 Richard Thompson Floyd, NYT Room for Debate (May 12, 2016)

special interests? At the same time, congressional representatives have the opportunity to advocate for these things, as well. If American voters insist on this break from corrupt democracy and crony capitalism in their selection of a candidate, the beginnings of change can emerge.

Most of all, in this and future elections, the electorate's ability to objectively evaluate candidates' and their representative supporters' platforms and priorities for change will determine whether or not America finds principled compromise for all or populist tyranny for the few. Historically, Americans have avoided tyranny by choosing well enough in elections. But the risks are great, and American voters are amateurs playing at a game that requires increased professionalism. This is not a problem that will be solved during this election cycle. A longer-term solution is to create citizen professionals: global citizen patriots.

The Long Way to Effective Democracy

Yuval Levin argues that moral formation is a long-term process. Is the formation of high-performing citizens any different? While we might agree in principle that effective representative democracy requires representatives and citizens to do their jobs and do them well, where are the training grounds that promote these ends? There are very few non-minimum-wage jobs that do not require some combination of significant technical expertise, emotional intelligence, and experience. Doctors, nurses, and medical technicians go to specialized medical schools for years, gain experience in residencies, and have continuing education requirements. Firefighters and police have well-defined initial and ongoing training standards that must be met. The military imposes a wide range of basic and ongoing physical, mental, and technical require-ments as part of its extensive training regimens. Corporations recruit a wide range of marketing, sales, computing, finance and accounting, research, communication, technical, scientific, and other talent and then provide ongoing firm-specific training and experience designed to increase employee value and productivity. College professors endure rigorous degree requirements and the scrutiny of peers before they can attain tenured status. Electricians, plumbers, and other trades are sub-ject to licensing, apprenticeships, and ongoing training in order to do their jobs. So why is it that we expect citizens to competently perform the job of citizenship—a job that is ill defined, has few requirements, and requires little formal education or training?

American citizenship is currently more an accident of birthplace than a position to be earned. The primary and secondary education systems provide at least some education on the history, structures, and respon-sibilities of democracy. However, where is the regular, ongoing curricu-lum that qualifies and requires citizens to perform? How many current citizens could actually pass the tests administered to immigrants who wish to become US citizens? How can citizens become more aware of the importance of sustaining and developing our five capital resources? Are there conditions beyond felony convictions that should suspend or disqualify citizen status? What rewards are there for being a better citizen—a global citizen patriot?

Perhaps our demos (our organization of citizens) is similar to any other organization in that, over time, the organization becomes what it rewards. If we believe that effective citizenship is the core of a well-func-tioning democracy, then we should consider both what we want citizens to do and provide them with rewards (and perhaps penalties) that will make it so.

Creating and Rewarding Global Citizen Patriots

A previous chapter, "Desperately Seeking Global Citizen Patriots," described mainstream America's inability to see itself objectively. The inability to overcome long-held "myths of America" combined with bias to return to the illusion of better historical times are failures of media, the education system, and our representatives to objectively present information. Moreover, these myths persist in an environment where alarming numbers of Americans are simply not paying attention. America's system of constitutional values, democracy, and capitalism has much to be proud of. Our capital resources are second to none. But where is the leadership that frees America from the gridlock and corruption of special interests? Where are the ideas and suggested reforms that will ensure that we adequately serve the long-term interests of all Americans, play the role that only America can in ensuring global security, and serve as a model society that attracts others to our system? The right questions, the alternatives, and potential solutions exist. There is a real, not mythical, America that can be discovered by global citizen patriots. But this will take continuous effort, resources, and accountability.

It has taken this author over three years of work to create a base of understanding; in essence, this project has been a lesson in civics that has yielded the confidence to suggest many of the important questions that America needs to address in order for our system to adapt and progress. Further, certain beliefs have been reinforced. These include not only the belief that our present system is dysfunctional, but that the solutions lie in forward, not backward, thinking. Most of all, it seems obvious that our current state requires us to deliberate and try various approaches. The status quo benefits only those who benefit from the present system of dysfunction.

How can an ongoing ability to assess and execute the right changes at the right times be made a part of our constitutional, democratic, and capitalistic system? We can get the money out of the election process, and reduce the ability of special interests to influence policy. But what is the role of citizens in creating the ongoing changes needed to progress? Can uninformed and disengaged citizens elect the right representatives and hold them accountable? Unlikely. What can be done to create activist, informed citizens who are accountable for America's future? There is no one single solution or right answer to this. But there are ideas and processes of discussion and selection that can yield consensus ways forward. Here are a few basic suggestions to foster debate and, in the process, begin the long-term formation of global citizen patriots.

Informed and engaged citizens are foundational to an effective and contemporary democracy. Let's consider ideas that will encourage and support citizens' ability to do the job of citizenship. For example:

- Revise primary and secondary education curricula to include, every year, a mandatory graded course that steadily educates our future citizens about the history and operation of each element of our three-tiered system, the system's role in enhancing our nation's five capital assets (with a particular focus on human capital development), the roles and responsibilities of citizens and their representatives, the historical and current sources and uses of government monies and the programs they support, and a broad treatment of ongoing policy areas (poverty, crime, security, environment, community, international relations, etc.). Students should be regularly tested on their grasp on the facts and the concepts as well as their ability to critically think about the issues. At the conclusion of secondary education, we should be assured that citizens have the information, knowledge, and critical thinking skills to perform as citizens.

- Award future citizenship not at birth but only after primary and secondary students complete the coursework. Immigrants (and those who do not complete secondary education) wishing to become citizens would be required to go through a condensed but comprehensive curriculum, pass an examination, and submit to appropriate security screening. Existing citizens would be grandfathered but encouraged to self-study the secondary-level curriculum. While this would require a very gradual transition (approximately 18 years for the typical student), it would immediately send the message that citizenship has to be earned.

- Require our tertiary education system to offer credit-bearing electives that further develop the coursework done at the secondary level. The purpose of these electives would be to provide additional depth to students' understanding of the system and the issues and involve them in increasingly sophisticated debate. These electives would also be an early indicator of student interest in playing a role as a representative at the state or national level.

- Revoke citizenship for persistent failure to vote, felony conviction, failure to perform military or equivalent public service, or pay taxes (with appropriate restoration methods).

- Reward citizenship as an important position that is earned through education and performance. Let's consider tying Social Security and Medicare (but not Medicaid) benefits to active citizen status rather than employment status (note that this will require a discussion of revoking the arguably regressive payroll tax and replacing it with revised income or VAT tax). All citizens should enjoy basic retirement and health benefits that are independent of employment. Stay-at-home parents and those unable to work due to age, disability, or for other valid reasons still need to perform as citizens. The job of citizenship has value that should be concretely recognized. What gets rewarded gets done.

These suggestions would provide teeth to our current citizenship requirements and responsibilities. Some of these may be a bridge too far—careful debate and discussion is essential. Regardless, if we expect citizens to perform at a higher level than at present, some meaningful changes need to occur. Changes to citizen information, education, and incentives (and penalties) can make a difference in the performance of citizens—and serve as the foundation for global citizen patriots.

The Constitutional Debates

Many of the suggestions made herein involve changes that touch on constitutional issues. Campaign financing rules, voter rights and districting, and eligibility for citizenship are only a few examples. Amending the Constitution is not a core competency of American democracy. As retired Supreme Court Justice John Paul Stevens has noted, "the proce-dures for amending the Constitution set forth in Article V have been successfully employed only eighteen times during the nation's history. On the first occasion, the ten amendments described as the Bill of Rights were all adopted at once."[2] It is astounding that our last consti-tutional amendment was in 1992! Since that time, the Supreme Court, rather than a deliberative legislative process, has determined campaign financing rules, the composition of Congress and state legislatures, and positions on important social issues such as the death penalty, the defi-nition of marriage, and the regulation of firearms. Have we defaulted to a system where a very small number of lawyers are forced to make decisions that should be made by citizens and their representatives? What about issues that never reach the Supreme Court? Congressional gridlock prevents actions on infrastructure improvement, environmen-tal issues, reform of social and work-related programs, tax simplifica-tion and reform, and most other important policy issues. Our founders faced many of the same issues as they constructed the rules that became our Constitution and Bill of Rights. The vehicle they used to debate and resolve the many questions was a constitutional convention.

It's time to consider amending our Constitution in a comprehensive way. Rather than having partisan representatives (beholden to biasing interests) endlessly debate individual amendments to no conclusion, it is time for what Professor Lessig refers to as "an intervention, from people, from friends, **from outside**"[3] (emphasis added by the author). Professor Lessig goes on to suggest a modern-day constitutional

---

2 John Paul Stevens, *Six Amendments: How and Why We Should Change the Constitution* (New York, Little, Brown and Company, 2014), p. 5

3 Lessig, p. 291

convention that will instigate debate across a wide range of constitutional issues. Noting the difficulty of accomplishing this in today's political environment, Lessig concludes that state-by-state conventions are the best hope for dialogue that excludes existing congressional and state representatives. He proposes that these conventions be "a citizens' movement only"[4] that "should not be a convention of experts. Or politicians. Or activists. It should be a convention of randomly selected voters called to a process of informed deliberation, who then concur on proposals that would be carried to the states. Delegates would have their salaries and expenses covered by the convention."[5]

Prior to these conventions, Lessig proposes the creation of state-by-state or regional "deliberative polls" of a representative sample of the general citizenry[6] that will map out how the conventions should work and determine the issues to be covered. "The aim of a deliberative poll is not just to figure out what people think. The aim instead is to figure out what people would think if they were well informed enough about the matter that they were being polled about....providing participants with the information they need to speak sensibly about the matter they are addressing."[7] Since the information used to inform these polls is obviously critical to the results, media and academia should play roles in creating and fact-checking the material that conventioneers will rely on. The eventual outcome of these "shadow conventions" would be to push enough of the states (approval by thirty-four states is necessary to call a federal-level convention) to support a national convention, a

---

4 Ibid., p. 301

5 Ibid., p 303

6 Ibid., p 302

7 Ibid.

true constitutional convention. This would be great reality television for twenty-first-century global citizen patriots!

Initially, it would seem wise to focus these deliberative polls and the subsequent conventions on constitutional issues and perhaps even consider limiting those to a digestible number. Much work has already been done in identifying potential constitutional amendment areas. For example, in *Six Amendments: How and Why We Should Change the Constitution*, John Paul Stevens offers six areas for amendment. These are: the anti-commandeering rule (dealing with the balance of responsibilities and power between the federal government and the states), political gerrymandering, campaign finance, sovereign immunity, the death penalty, and the Second Amendment (as it pertains to gun control).[8] Stevens's suggested areas would be excellent fodder for the polls and the conventions, combining areas essential to dealing with the corruption of our representatives with issues of great public interest. In addition to Stevens's six, it would seem logical to deal with congressional terms, the responsibilities of representatives, and their compensation and performance accountabilities as part of these debates. At a minimum, these conventions need to recommend the means to get the best possible future representatives and ensure that they work only on behalf of citizens. The convention process will make a fundamental difference only if it reforms campaign financing, campaign contributions, and the terms and conditions that determine the responsibilities, term limits, accountabilities, and rewards of representatives.

---

8 Stevens, p. vii

No doubt there will be significant resistance from entrenched special interests and from those who view the Constitution as an immutable, nearly sacred document. However, given the high levels of interest in the current election as shown in the large audiences for the Republican and Democratic debates and in the significant primary voter turnouts, it is easy to imagine a citizenry that would be empowered and enthused by the idea of a modern-day convention. Perhaps Donald Trump would find that conventions provide a road map for policies that enjoy popular support and provide direction to his frequently changing views on many issues. Or perhaps Bernie Sanders and Hillary Clinton can find in the convention outcomes positions that will merge their disagreements into a consensus direction. Perhaps conventions will give voice to third parties. While the election will occur before conventions can be organized and executed, commitment to conventions from either or both parties' candidates could be an important differentiator in the election.

While deliberative conventions seem logical to Lessig (and to the author), it is still possible that this may be a bit too much reality television for many Americans. If so, let's at least consider some form of deliberative debate to test the concept and work out problems. For example, if enough momentum cannot be generated for state-level debates, let's start by asking volunteer universities to sponsor test debates on constitutional and policy issues. Using the same random citizen selection and deliberative polling suggested by Lessig, these forums would ideally serve as proof of concept and provide advice on the best ways to extend it to the state level. The potential gains to the sponsoring universities in terms of visibility and reputation, as well as the learning opportunities for their students, seem obvious.

The Policy Debates

Beyond constitutional issues, there are a wide range of policy areas where Congress has failed to act. These issues are complex and contextual. For example, issues relating to budgets, fiscal prudence, and investment have to be viewed in the context of country-specific and worldwide economic conditions. Does it make sense to invest more in infrastructure and R&D during good economic times? Should more money be spent on job creation and human capital development during economic downturns or times of technology-driven employment disruption? How, and how fast, do we adapt our environmental policies to ensure a sustainable, and even better, environment? What are the best ways to determine the optimal size of the nation's economic pie and each of its slices? In short, how do we use the nation's wealth in support of the greatest good for the greatest number over the longest term?

There are several areas that are fundamental to the adaptation and enhancement of our constitutional values, democracy, and capitalism. Many of these are not constitutional issues, but they are either strategic prerequisites for change or societal priorities. These include:

- How can we balance what we want with what we can afford? Let's revisit how we source and use public funds. At present, our annual spending deficits and long-term national debt seem unsustainable barring unrealistic projections of future growth and productivity. If this is the case, what are the alternatives that balance increased taxes, spending cuts in certain areas, and investments to spur growth? The inability of our representatives to craft this grand bargain is currently very costly. In its 2011 *Going for*

Growth report, the Organisation for Economic Co-operation and Development (OECD) estimated that changes to our health care, education, and environmental policies could produce cost savings totaling 4.6% of GDP.[9] In addition, the OECD identified tax reform opportunities to increase tax revenues while maintaining the country's position with relatively low taxes as a percentage of GDP when compared with other developed countries.[10] The OECD's analysis suggests that there are meaningful opportunities to get our financial house in order and invest in the future.

- How can we ensure that American demography is managed strategically rather than emotionally? Given current birth rates and levels of emigration and immigration, we risk an inadequate future supply of working-age people. Ruchir Sharma has stated that the US labor force is "growing very slowly—at 0.5 percent over the past decade, compared with 1.7 percent from 1960 to 2005."[11] This is important if Sharma is correct that "a one-percentage-point decline in the population growth rate will eventually reduce the economic growth rate by roughly a percentage point." Perhaps candidate Trump should consider this before deporting 11,000,000 predominantly young immigrants—would we be better off integrating them into the economy? Further, how can we ease our visa and work requirements to attract the best and brightest talent? If human capital is our single most important asset, and the critical determinant of future growth, let's create immigration and job creation policies accordingly.

---

9 OECD Report, pp. 38-47

10 Ibid., p. 44

11 Ruchir Sharma, "The Demographics of Stagnation," *Foreign Affairs* (March/April 2016) p. 18

- Do we support and help enforce the principles of the universal statements of human rights and human responsibilities? If so, what are the best ways for America to collaborate with like-minded countries and others in terms of, for example, disaster relief, military intervention, poverty alleviation, development and trade, and international governance, legal and regulatory, and financial systems? America's legacy and future success will depend in part on its ability to be a principled leader that uses its resources to advance and secure progress everywhere, even when it means sacrifice at the national level. Isolationism is not an option in an interdependent world. But how do we want to participate?

- What are the best ways to build an inclusive and effective society that addresses the challenges posed by single parenting, high child poverty rates, very unequal education opportunities, changing gender and sexual norms, inadequate jobs, an aging population, communities segregated by wealth, and so on? A patchwork of government, philanthropic, volunteer, and other approaches cannot expect to fix such an extensive set of problems. Enhanced social capital requires a comprehensive strategy that offers basic protections and high-quality opportunities for all.

There are many other issues that can be considered strategic challenges; for example, sustaining and enhancing our natural capital, and maintaining and enhancing our built capital. All of these are complex topics with many alternative possible solutions. Choosing wisely is difficult. But if we fail to holistically debate the alternatives, are unable to create compromise between the perceived winners and the losers, and are unwilling or unable to try different solutions, we will certainly fail to change.

Elections, conventions, and university-sponsored debates are some of the tools that can help form professional citizens. Overcoming the influence of money on representatives is a critical first step. But the long-term legacy of America will be determined, as it has been historically, through the preferences and guidance of its citizens. Are we willing to pledge ourselves to a new level of global patriotic citizenship that will provide that direction?

The Global Citizen Patriot Pledge

The notion of well-informed, activist, critically thinking citizens with a global perspective can only be an ideal, a goal that is ever-evolving in the face of a changing world. As stated earlier, it is beyond the capacity of citizens to understand and engage with every issue that requires attention. We can only hold our representatives accountable to their responsibility to order and determine on our behalf the responses that will best fit the needs of society. This book has suggested ways that these representatives' roles, responsibilities, and accountabilities have to be restructured. Representative reform is the necessary first requirement for changes that will defeat corrupted democracy and crony capitalism. But this reform is insufficient. In the long run, only a nation of global citizen patriots can ensure that our representative's proposals are true to the vision and values of our founders while adapting to contemporary opportunities and challenges.

All Americans are familiar with The Pledge of Allegiance but are less aware that it has been altered four times since its initial composition in 1887 by Colonel George Balch. The most current version was last changed in 1954. Let's consider enhancing the pledge to better articulate the roles and responsibilities of a new generation of high-performing citizens—global citizen patriots.

Americans treasure individual freedom and benefit from diversity of thought. One person's interpretation of good citizenship is only that— one person's opinion. But this individualism and diversity of thought is best harnessed on behalf of all when citizens and their representatives pledge to:

- Ask and debate basic questions of values and value to ensure that citizens have informed views that promote collective patriotism versus partisan conflict. **Pledge to be an informed and activist citizen.**

- Participate in the adaptation of our representative democracy to better support our values and create value for all, contribute to global security and development, and find the best balance between lollipops for all and Darwinian survival of the fittest. **Pledge to engage in debate, vote, and collaborate through compromise.**

- Ensure that our form of capitalism builds and sustains all of America's capital resources, contributes to societal enhancement, and performs as a valid market economy with appropriate moral and ethical limits. **Pledge to oppose forces that waste, fail to develop, or misuse any of our five capital assets and hold representatives accountable to manage the wealth of our nation.**

- Extend America's resources and capabilities globally to promote development, security, and the values that underpin the American Dream. Our neighbors are not just those within our borders. **Pledge to honor the legacy of those who made the ultimate sacrifice on behalf of our country and our global neighbors by supporting sacrifices today that hope to avoid more costly sacrifices later.**

America's system of constitutional values, democracy, and capitalism is subject to increasing criticism both at home and abroad. We are mad as hell because we know that the system is rigged in favor of a small and powerful minority. However, when the system functions on behalf of all, it has proven to be an enduring and powerful way to construct a society. How can we take back the system and return it to its rightful owners—American citizens? Global citizen patriots and their representatives are the only arbiters that can update our values and clarify what we value. They are the only force that can ensure that our representatives work for the greatest good for the greatest number over the longest term. And they are the ones who will be most positively impacted by a reformed democracy and capitalism that works not just for the powerful and connected few but for the entire society. Let's ensure that 50 years from now, future citizens will look back at this time as a revitalization of America rather than reflect on a lost empire and wonder, what were they thinking?

Let's engage, vote, and initiate the discussions necessary to ensure that the legacy of present-day Americans lives up to the vision and values of our founders. It is up to us. An enlightened and activist majority of global citizen patriots can be a sixth capital asset and an enduring advantage in creating a better future.

CHAPTER 8:
QUO VADIS? READER INPUT AND DISCUSSION

Where are we going? Reader input.

Reader Input: Share Your Thoughts

Readers are encouraged to join the debate via globalcitizenpatriots.com. Your reactions, ideas, and questions can be offered publicly through provided links to Facebook and LinkedIn. Using these links will enable ongoing dialogue. In addition, those who wish to provide private input can send the author an e-mail to jmregan3@gmail.com. The author will reply to e-mail and social media as time permits.

There are no rules for this dialogue other than all comments should be supported by evidence and facts as possible. The author respectfully submits this book with awareness that certain findings and suggestions will be disputed. Your equally respectful comments, ideas, and disagreements are welcome.

Getting Started

A few years ago, the author had the privilege of addressing the 2014 graduating students of his high school alma mater. My remarks focused on many of the concerns and questions raised in this book. As a way of starting the dialogue with something provocative, below is one small piece of that speech.

"How can we reorder our priorities to ensure opportunity and basic security for all?"

This is often framed as a provocative debate about inequality. Do the CEOs of multinational corporations make too much money? How about hedge fund managers, the top twenty-five of whom in 2013 took home $21.15 billion? These are great questions for shareholder activists, hedge fund investors, and the media. But are they the right questions for mainstream citizens more focused on opportunities for advancement? Will limits on executive pay address the plight of the less fortunate? I doubt it. A better question: is there sufficient wealth to address basic needs worldwide and adopt policies that promise opportunity for all? In fact, citizens do have a menu of choices, the costs and benefits of which need to be understood if they are to align societal needs with the policies of their representatives. Two examples might help illustrate this. In a 2010 article, Anup Shah listed some of the world's annual consumption priorities. These included $8 billion for cosmetics in the United States, $50 billion for cigarettes in the EU, $400 billion for narcotic drugs worldwide, and, the big one, $780 billion for worldwide military spending. Contrast these spending priorities with the estimated $40 billion total cost to provide basic education, water and sanitation, reproductive health services for all women, and health and nutrition for all the world's needy. You heard me correctly, only $40 billion annually. I ask: do we have an income distribution problem or a spending priorities problem? Perhaps both. It can be addressed if we citizens so insist.

My second example derives from the fact that most developed countries, as documented in the Copenhagen Consensus Project, spend as much as 99% of their GDP on themselves. What collective responsibility do we have to redirect country-specific spending and tax receipts to ensure that all have the education, nutrition, health, security from violence, and unbiased information that are the essential foundations of opportunity and societal stability? It is wonderful to see the Gates Foundation and Warren Buffett, and the Chinese businessmen Jack Ma and Joseph Tsai, cofounders of Alibaba, redirect large amounts of their business-generated wealth to global causes. However, whether through philanthropic, government, or private aid, enhanced free trade or provision of services (such as military assistance), rich countries, communities, and individuals need to better serve the poor and undeveloped everywhere. It is in every citizen's interest."

Graduation speeches (and speakers!) quickly fade from graduates' minds as they turn to their next challenges. In the author's case, however, this speech served as the foundation for the notion of global citizen patriots and how they might better address the frustrations that make Americans mad as hell. This book makes the case for citizen activism in the short term that will result in elections that are financed only with public money and small contributions for large numbers of donors. At the same time, changes to the responsibilities, term limits, and rewards of our elected representatives can help ensure they work as leaders in securing the public interest. In the long run, let's redefine the roles and responsibilities of citizens and provide them with the information, skills, and reward incentives that will ensure the creation of a professional citizenry. These ideas are the essential thesis of this book. What do you think? What is missed? What are your questions, concerns, ideas, and suggestions?

Let's hear from you!

GREATEST HITS

Greatest Hits Explained

One of the advantages of retirement is that you have time. For the last four years, I devoted several hours most days attempting to determine whether in fact it is possible for citizens to acquire enough knowledge to perform the duties of citizenship in an informed manner. Since I was unable to find curricula or any single source that provides a road map, I relied on over 200 books, approximately 1,000 articles and reports, and content gathered from meetings and presentations to inform my research. While this process was somewhat random, I did have the advantage of completing the graduate Master of Arts program at the Fletcher School of Law and Diplomacy in 2006. This coursework, in addition to providing its advertised "global perspective," also helped identify respected, objective sources and map out the playing field of issues that one might consider.

Since not everyone has either the time or the interest to take on such an ambitious self-education effort, I have boiled these sources down to my "greatest hits" (and several honorable mentions). My first list is books, to be followed in the future with lists of articles, reports, and presentations that I found to be compelling and important to the concept of global citizen patriots. I hope that you find these helpful.

Global Citizen Patriots' Must-Read Books

The books listed here (in no particular order) are remarkable aids to the education of global citizen patriots. While in total they are not comprehensive in scope, they represent a great starting point. My criteria for inclusion are simple: are they readable, do they instruct on issues or concepts important to citizen performance, and do they attempt to be both fact-based and objective? The full list is provided in the bibliography. I hope that you find this helpful, and I look forward to your recommended additions.

The Price of Civilization by Jeffrey Sachs. So many great books by Sachs—an economist with a social conscience! This book is comprehensive in its economic and social analyses and in its prescriptions for change. You may not agree with everything Sachs says, but he certainly offers a wide perspective for debate. You may also want to read his previous efforts: *Common Wealth* and *The End of Poverty*.

Republic, Lost: How Money Corrupts Congress—and a Plan to Stop It by Lawrence Lessig. The essential primer on congressional corruption with Lessig's prescriptions for change. If this doesn't make you "mad as hell," you are citizen, lost.

The Gardens of Democracy: A New American Story of Citizenship, the Economy, and the Role of Government by Eric Liu and Nick Hanauer. A concise description of the failure of "either/or" thinking;

suggestions to update American ideals, citizen performance, and relevance, economic principles, and the roles of government.

What Is Citizenship? by Derek Heater. Citizenship 101; a description of liberal versus civic republican traditions, definitions, problems, and proposed resolutions.

What's the Economy For, Anyway? Why It's Time to Stop Chasing Growth and Start Pursuing Happiness by John de Graaf and David Batker. Producing more and consuming more does not automatically ensure the greatest good for the largest number over the long run. The authors debunk many of the popular myths about America and suggest ways to refocus our economy on policies that will improve "life, liberty, and happiness." Honorable mention to Michael Sandel's *What Money Can't Buy: The Moral Limits of Markets,* a concise description of the moral and ethical questions we need to consider in order to balance markets and societal values.

Models of Democracy by David Held. For anyone who thinks of democracy as a uniform concept. We have choices as to the form our democracy needs to take in the modern world. Held thoroughly lays out the various models and offers a proposed model for our time.

Capital in the Twenty-First Century by Thomas Piketty. Read this if you missed macroeconomics in high school or college. Or read this because you need the facts on global inequality. This masterpiece is the essential history lesson on the economics surrounding inequality combined with compelling data.

Empire: The Rise and Demise of the British World Order and the Lessons for Global Power by Niall Ferguson. The opportunity of empire and how to use power to create a better world. The example of Britain and lessons for the United States are thought provoking.

Political Order and Political Decay: From the Industrial Revolution to the Globalization of Democracy by Francis Fukuyama. The lessons of political history in an incredibly comprehensive and thoughtful work. This is a loud warning to America concerning the current state of its democracy and its future.

Citizens Divided: Campaign Finance Reform and the Constitution by Robert Post. Let the constitutional debates begin, starting with the failure of the US Congress to deal with issues essential to societal progress. This is a convincing view of the sources of corruption that cause representative failure. Spoiler alert: constitutional changes required! Honorable mention on this topic goes to former Chief Justice of the US Supreme Court John Paul Stevens for his *Six Amendments: How and Why We Should Change the Constitution.*

So Damn Much Money: The Triumph of Lobbying and the Corrosion of American Government by Robert Kaiser. Also on the subject of congressional corruption, Kaiser's detective work illuminates how money and the proliferation of lobbyists, political consultants, captive media, and captive academics distort the performance of congressional representatives in ways that make it clear who they actually work for. Terrifying.

The Post-American World by Fareed Zakaria. The essential cheat sheet for Americans who need to better understand non-Western mind-sets, cultures, and values; the basic global perspectives needed by Americans if we are to better, and more positively, influence ongoing globalization.

Reinventing Fire: Bold Business Solutions for the New Energy Era by Amory Lovins and the Rocky Mountain Institute. Clean energy science for non-scientific types like me. Everything you need to know about energy sources, costs, and the market reforms needed to ensure adequate and clean energy.

The Second Machine Age: Work, Progress, and Prosperity in a Time of Brilliant Technologies by Erik Brynjolfsson and Andrew McAfee. The development of advanced forms of artificial intelligence will have a profound effect on the future of work and jobs. This is a practical guide to individual and aggregate changes that can help mitigate this societal disruption. This book made me glad to be in retirement!

The Politics of Happiness: What Government Can Learn from the New Research on Well-Being by Derek Bok. Bok enlightens the squishy topic of "happiness" with facts and analyses that objectively discuss the false choice between policies to increase economic growth versus policies to increase citizen well-being.

BIBLIOGRAPHY

Altinay, Hakan, ed. *Global Civics: Responsibilities and Rights in an Interdependent World*. Washington, D.C.: Brookings Institution, 2011. Print.

Ariely, Dan. *Predictably Irrational: The Hidden Forces That Shape Our Decisions*. New York: HarperCollins, 2008. Print.

Austin, James E. *Managing in Developing Countries: Strategic Analysis and Operating Techniques*. New York: Free Press, 1990. Print.

Baer, Robert. *Sleeping with the Devil: How Washington Sold Our Soul for Saudi Crude*. New York: Crown, 2003. Print.

Baumol, William J., Robert E. Litan, and Carl J. Schramm. *Good Capitalism, Bad Capitalism, and the Economics of Growth and Prosperity*. New Haven: Yale University Press, 2007. Print.

Bederman, David J. *International Law Frameworks*. New York: Foundation, 2001. Print.

Bell, Daniel. *The Coming of Post-Industrial Society; a Venture in Social Forecasting*. New York: Basic, 1973. Print.

Berger, Suzanne, and the MIT Industrial Performance Center. *How We Compete: What Companies around the World Are Doing to Make It in Today's Global Economy.* New York: Currency Doubleday, 2006. Print.

Betts, Richard K. *American Force: Dangers, Delusions, and Dilemmas in National Security.* New York: Columbia University Press, 2012. Print.

Bishop, Matthew, and Michael Green. *Philanthro-capitalism: How the Rich Can Save the World.* New York: Bloomsbury, 2009. Print.

Bok, Derek Curtis. *The Politics of Happiness: What Government Can Learn from the New Research on Well-Being.* Princeton, NJ: Princeton University Press, 2010. Print.

Bremmer, Ian. *The End of the Free Market: Who Wins the War between States and Corporations?* New York: Portfolio, 2010. Print.

Breslin, J. William, and Jeffrey Z. Rubin. *Negotiation Theory and Practice.* Cambridge, MA: Program on Negotiation at Harvard Law School, 1995. Print.

Brewer, Thomas L., Kenneth H. David, and Linda Lim. *Investing in Developing Countries: A Guide for Executives.* Lexington, MA: Lexington, 1986. Print.

Brooks, Stephen G. *Producing Security: Multinational Corporations, Globalization, and the Changing Calculus of Conflict.* Princeton, NJ: Princeton University Press, 2005. Print.

Brynjolfsson, Erik, and Andrew McAfee. *The Second Machine Age: Work, Progress, and Prosperity in a Time of Brilliant Technologies.* New York: W. W. Norton, 2014. Print.

Calleo, David P. *Follies of Power: America's Unipolar Fantasy.* Cambridge: Cambridge University Press, 2009. Print.

Chang, Ha-Joon. *23 Things They Don't Tell You about Capitalism.* New York: Bloomsbury, 2010. Print.

Chayes, Sarah. *Thieves of State: Why Corruption Threatens Global Security.* New York: W. W. Norton, 2015. Print.

Chernow, Ron. *Alexander Hamilton.* New York: Penguin, 2004. Print.

Chua, Amy. *World on Fire: How Exporting Free Market Democracy Breeds Ethnic Hatred and Global Instability.* New York: Doubleday, 2003. Print.

Cohen, Stephen D. *Multinational Corporations and Foreign Direct Investment: Avoiding Simplicity, Embracing Complexity.* Oxford: Oxford University Press, 2007. Print.

Collier, Paul. *The Bottom Billion: Why the Poorest Countries Are Failing and What Can Be Done about It.* Oxford: Oxford University Press, 2007. Print.

Cooke, William N. *Multinational Companies and Global Human Resource Strategies.* Westport, CT: Quorum, 2003. Print.

Cowen, Tyler. *Average Is Over: Powering America beyond the Age of the Great Stagnation.* New York: Dutton, 2013. Print.

Cowen, Tyler. *The Great Stagnation: How America Ate All the Low-Hanging Fruit of Modern History, Got Sick, and Will (Eventually) Feel Better.* New York: Dutton, 2011. Print.

Dawisha, Karen. *Putin's Kleptocracy: Who Owns Russia?* New York: Simon & Schuster, 2014. Print.

Dionne, E. J. *Why the Right Went Wrong: Conservatism—From Goldwater to the Tea Party and Beyond.* New York: Simon & Schuster, 2016. Print.

Easterly, William. *The White Man's Burden: Why the West's Efforts to Aid the Rest Have Done so Much Ill and so Little Good.* New York: Penguin, 2006. Print.

Evans, Peter B. *Dependent Development: The Alliance of Multinational, State, and Local Capital in Brazil.* Princeton, NJ: Princeton University Press, 1979. Print.

Feinstein, Lee, and Tod Lindberg. *Means to an End: U.S. Interest in the International Criminal Court.* Washington, D.C.: Brookings Institution, 2009. Print.

Ferguson, Niall. *Empire: The Rise and Demise of the British World Order and the Lessons for Global Power.* New York: Basic, 2003. Print.

Ferguson, Niall. *The Great Degeneration: How Institutions Decay and Economies Die*. New York: Penguin Group, 2012. Print.

Fleishman, Joel L. *The Foundation: A Great American Secret: How Private Wealth Is Changing the World*. New York: PublicAffairs, 2007. Print.

Friedman, Thomas L. *The Lexus and the Olive Tree*. New York: Farrar, Straus, Giroux, 1999. Print.

Friedman, Thomas L. *Longitudes and Attitudes: The World in the Age of Terrorism*. New York: Anchor, 2003. Print.

Friedman, Thomas L. *The World Is Flat: A Brief History of the Twenty-First Century*. New York: Farrar, Straus and Giroux, 2005. Print.

Fukuyama, Francis. *Political Order and Political Decay: From the Industrial Revolution to the Globalization of Democracy*. New York: Farrar, Straus, and Giroux, 2014. Print.

George, Alexander L. *Forceful Persuasion: Coercive Diplomacy as an Alternative to War*. Washington, D.C.: United States Institute of Peace, 1991. Print.

Graaf, John de, and David K. Batker. *What's the Economy For, Anyway?: Why It's Time to Stop Chasing Growth and Start Pursuing Happiness*. New York: Bloomsbury, 2011. Print.

Graham, Edward M. *Multinationals and Foreign Investment in Economic Development*. Houndmills, Basingstoke, Hampshire: Palgrave Macmillan, 2005. Print.

Heater, Derek Benjamin. *What Is Citizenship?* Malden, MA: Polity, 1999. Print.

Johnson, Paul. *Modern Times: A History of the World from the 1920s to the 1990s*. London: Phoenix, 1992. Print.

Kaiser, Robert G. *So Damn Much Money: The Triumph of Lobbying and the Corrosion of American Government*. New York: Knopf, 2009. Print.

Kaldor, Mary. *New and Old Wars: Organized Violence in a Global Era*. Stanford, CA: Stanford University Press, 1999. Print.

Kennedy, Paul M. *The Rise and Fall of the Great Powers: Economic Change and Military Conflict from 1500 to 2000*. New York: Random House, 1987. Print.

Kling, Arnold S. *Crisis of Abundance: Rethinking How We Pay for Health Care*. Washington, D.C.: Cato Institute, 2006. Print.

Kling, Arnold S., and Nick Schulz. *From Poverty to Prosperity: Intangible Assets, Hidden Liabilities, and the Lasting Triumph over Scarcity*. New York: Encounter, 2009. Print.

Kotkin, Joel. *The Next Hundred Million: America in 2050.* New York: Penguin, 2010. Print.

Kotter, John P. *Leading Change.* Boston, MA: Harvard Business School, 1996. Print.

Kristof, Nicholas D., and Sheryl WuDunn. *Half the Sky: Turning Oppression into Opportunity for Women Worldwide.* New York: Alfred A. Knopf, 2009. Print.

Lessig, Lawrence. *Republic, Lost: How Money Corrupts Congress—and a Plan to Stop It.* New York: Twelve, 2011. Print.

Levin, Mark R. *The Liberty Amendments: Restoring the American Republic.* New York: Simon & Schuster, 2013. Print.

Lewis, William W. *The Power of Productivity: Wealth, Poverty, and the Threat to Global Stability.* Chicago: U of Chicago, 2004. Print.

Liu, Eric, and Nick Hanauer. *The Gardens of Democracy: A New American Story of Citizenship, the Economy, and the Role of Government.* Seattle, WA: Sasquatch, 2011. Print.

Lomborg, Bjørn. *How Much Have Global Problems Cost the World?: A Scorecard from 1900 to 2050.* New York: Cambridge University Press, 2013. Print.

Lomborg, Bjørn. *How to Spend $75 Billion to Make the World a Better Place.* Washington, D.C.: Copenhagen Consensus Center, 2013. Print.

Lovins, Amory B. *Reinventing Fire: Bold Business Solutions for the New Energy Era.* White River Junction, VT: Chelsea Green, 2011. Print.

Mandelbaum, Michael. *The Frugal Superpower: America's Global Leadership in a Cash-Strapped Era.* New York: PublicAffairs, 2010. Print.

Martenson, Chris. *The Crash Course: The Unsustainable Future of Our Economy, Energy, and Environment.* Hoboken, NJ: John Wiley and Sons, 2011. Print.

Mauldin, John, and Jonathan Tepper. *Endgame: The End of the Debt Supercycle and How It Changes Everything.* Hoboken, NJ: John Wiley, 2011. Print.

Mayer, Jane. *Dark Money: The Hidden History of the Billionaires behind the Rise of the Radical Right.* New York: Doubleday, 2016. Print.

McGinnis, John O. *Accelerating Democracy: Transforming Governance through Technology.* Princeton, NJ: Princeton University Press, 2013. Print.

Meacham, Jon. *Thomas Jefferson: The Art of Power.* New York: Random House, 2012. Print.

Milanović, Branko. *The Haves and the Have-nots: A Brief and Idiosyncratic History of Global Inequality*. New York: Basic, 2011. Print.

Muller, Richard A. *Physics for Future Presidents: The Science behind the Headlines*. New York: W.W. Norton, 2008. Print.

Murray, Charles A. *Coming Apart: The State of White America, 1960– 2010*. New York: Crown Forum, 2012. Print.

Naím, Moisés. *The End of Power: From Boardrooms to Battlefields and Churches to States, Why Being in Charge Isn't What It Used to Be*. New York: Basic, 2013. Print.

Noah, Timothy. *The Great Divergence: America's Growing Inequality Crisis and What We Can Do about It*. New York: Bloomsbury, 2012. Print.

Noddings, Nel, ed. *Educating Citizens for Global Awareness*. New York: Teachers College, 2005. Print.

Oreskes, Naomi, and Erik M. Conway. *Merchants of Doubt: How a Handful of Scientists Obscured the Truth on Issues from Tobacco Smoke to Global Warming*. New York: Bloomsbury, 2010. Print.

Paine, Thomas. *Common Sense*. Edited by Isaac Kramnick. Harmondsworth Middlesex, England: Penguin, 1986. Print.

Pink, Daniel H. *Drive: The Surprising Truth about What Motivates Us*. New York: Riverhead, 2009. Print.

Porter, Gareth, Janet Welsh Brown, and Pamela S. Chasek. *Global Environmental Politics*. Boulder: Westview, 1991. Print.

Post, Robert. *Citizens Divided: Campaign Finance Reform and the Constitution*. Cambridge: Harvard University Press, 2014. Print.

Prahalad, C. K. *The Fortune at the Bottom of the Pyramid*. Upper Saddle River, NJ: Wharton School, 2006. Print.

Pruitt, Dean G., and Sung Hee Kim. *Social Conflict: Escalation, Stalemate, and Settlement*. New York: McGraw-Hill, 2003. Print.

Putnam, Robert D. *Our Kids: The American Dream in Crisis*. New York: Simon & Schuster, 2015. Print.

Rajan, Raghuram. *Fault Lines: How Hidden Fractures Still Threaten the World Economy*. Princeton, NJ: Princeton University Press, 2010. Print.

Reich, Robert B. *Supercapitalism: The Transformation of Business, Democracy, and Everyday Life*. New York: Alfred A. Knopf, 2007. Print.

Reich, Robert B. *The Work of Nations: Preparing Ourselves for 21st-Century Capitalism*. New York: A.A. Knopf, 1991. Print.

Rodrik, Dani. *The Globalization Paradox: Democracy and the Future of the World Economy*. New York: W.W. Norton, 2011. Print.

Rogers, Peter P., and Susan Leal. *Running Out of Water: The Looming Crisis and Solutions to Conserve Our Most Precious Resource*. New York: Palgrave Macmillan, 2010. Print.

Roubini, Nouriel. *Crisis Economics: A Crash Course in the Future of Finance*. New York: Penguin, 2010. Print.

Sachs, Jeffrey. *Common Wealth: Economics for a Crowded Planet*. New York: Penguin, 2008. Print.

Sachs, Jeffrey. *The End of Poverty: Economic Possibilities for Our Time*. New York: Penguin, 2005. Print.

Sachs, Jeffrey. *The Price of Civilization: Reawakening American Virtue and Prosperity*. New York: Random House, 2011. Print.

Salacuse, Jeswald W. *The Global Negotiator: Making, Managing, and Mending Deals around the World in the Twenty-First Century*. New York: Palgrave Macmillan, 2003. Print.

Sandel, Michael J. *What Money Can't Buy: The Moral Limits of Markets*. New York: Farrar, Straus and Giroux, 2012. Print.

Sharma, Ruchir. *Breakout Nations: In Pursuit of the Next Economic Miracles*. New York: W.W. Norton, 2012. Print.

Stern, Nicholas H. *A Strategy for Development*. Washington, D.C.: World Bank, 2002. Print.

Stevens, John Paul. *Six Amendments: How and Why We Should Change the Constitution.* New York: Little, Brown, 2014. Print.

Stiglitz, Joseph E. *The Stiglitz Report: Reforming the International Monetary and Financial Systems in the Wake of the Global Crisis.* New York: New, 2010. Print.

Stout, Lynn A. *The Shareholder Value Myth: How Putting Shareholders First Harms Investors, Corporations, and the Public.* San Francisco: Berrett-Koehler, 2012. Print.

Tavis, Lee A., and Timothy M. Tavis. *Values-Based Multinational Management: Achieving Enterprise Sustainability through a Human Rights Strategy.* Notre Dame, IN: U of Notre Dame, 2009. Print.

Taylor, Timothy. *America and the New Global Economy. Course Guidebook.* Chantilly, VA: Teaching, 2008. Print.

Wildavsky, Ben. *The Great Brain Race: How Global Universities Are Reshaping the World.* Princeton: Princeton University Press, 2010. Print.

Wirls, Daniel. *Irrational Security: The Politics of Defense from Reagan to Obama.* Baltimore, MD: Johns Hopkins University Press, 2010. Print.

Yergin, Daniel, and Joseph Stanislaw. *The Commanding Heights: The Battle for the World Economy.* New York: Simon & Schuster, 2002. Print.

Zakaria, Fareed. *The Future of Freedom: Illiberal Democracy at Home and Abroad.* New York: W.W. Norton, 2003. Print.

Zakaria, Fareed. *The Post-American World.* New York: W.W. Norton, 2008. Print.